CW00402690

Benedict XVI
and
Cardinal Newman

Edited by Peter Jennings

FAMILY PUBLICATIONS

OXFORD

© Family Publications, 2005

ISBN 1 871217 53 9

Addresses and sermons of the Holy Father as well as certain items
which appeared during his time as Prefect of the Congregation for the
Doctrine of Faith, Copyright © Libreria Editrice Vaticana.

cover illustrations

Benedict XVI during his Inaugural Mass
in St Peter's Square, 24 April 2005.
Fotografia Felici

Cardinal Newman by Sir John Everett Millais, 1881.
National Portrait Gallery, London

typeset and published by

FAMILY PUBLICATIONS
6A King Street, Jericho, Oxford OX2 6DF
www.familypublications.co.uk

printed in Malta

To Stella, Sarah and Joseph

and the Fathers of the Birmingham Oratory

for their encouragement over the years

Newman's Coat of Arms as Cardinal, original design.
Newman chose the motto *Cor ad Cor Loquitur*, 'Heart speaks to Heart'.

Courtesy of the Fathers of the Birmingham Oratory

Contents

Introduction

"Habemus Papam!" Cardinal Joseph Ratzinger, Dean of the College of Cardinals was elected as the Successor of Saint Peter, and Pontiff of the Roman Catholic Church on Tuesday afternoon, 19 April 2005. He chose the name Benedict XVI.

At 6.48 pm, a smiling Pope Benedict appeared on the central loggia of St Peter's Basilica. He spoke to the crowds who packed St Peter's Square and the surrounding streets:

> Dear Brothers and Sisters, after the great Pope John Paul II, the Cardinals have elected me, a simple and humble labourer in the vineyard of the Lord.

Pope Benedict XVI was elected on the fourth ballot by the 115 Cardinal Electors, who came from 52 countries. It would appear from interviews given afterwards by a number of cardinals who took part in the Conclave, that Cardinal Ratzinger received significantly more than the 76 votes, the two-thirds majority, required to be Pope.

When Cardinal Angelo Roncalli, Patriarch of Venice, was elected Pope John XXIII on 28 October 1958 he was 77 years old. At the time the media, because of his advanced age, described him as a 'caretaker' who was unlikely to do much during his Pontificate. He took everyone by surprise and called the Second Vatican Council, 1962-1965. The Papacy of Pope Benedict XVI, under the guidance of the Holy Spirit, will have its own marked style and be full of surprises!

The Catholic Church, and in particular the Vatican, captured the attention of the world's 24-hour media for more than a month early in 2005. It was headline news from the moment the health of Pope John Paul II deteriorated on Thursday 31 March. His death on Saturday 2 April and his Funeral Mass in St Peter's Square on Friday 8 April, attended by more than 200 world leaders, including the President of the United States of America, received unprecedented media coverage.

On Friday 1 April, the world's media focused their cameras on the Apostolic Palace, where Pope John Paul II lay dying. On that day Cardinal Joseph Ratzinger, who a week later was to preside and preach at the Funeral of Pope John Paul II, was at the Benedictine monastery of St Scholastica, in Subiaco, about 70 km east of Rome. It was here that St Benedict began his monastic life as a hermit. He eventually gathered about him a group of disciples and went to Monte Cassino where he wrote his Rule which, for nearly 1500 years, has provided the basis and structure of Western monasticism.

The purpose of Cardinal Ratzinger's visit to this ancient Benedictine abbey was to receive the St Benedict Award for the Promotion of Life and the Family in Europe, conferred by the Subiaco Foundation for Life and the Family. On this occasion Cardinal Ratzinger, Prefect of the Congregation for the Doctrine of the Faith, gave a challenging address during which he stressed: "Europe has developed a culture that, in a way previously unknown to humanity, excludes God from the public consciousness, either by denying him altogether or by judging that his existence cannot be demonstrated, is uncertain and, therefore, irrelevant to public life."

During his first General Audience in St Peter's Square on Wednesday, 27 April 2005, Pope Benedict XVI explained why he chose the name Benedict: "The name Benedict evokes the extraordinary figure of the great 'patriarch of western monasticism', St Benedict of Nursia, co-patron of Europe with Cyril and Methodius. The progressive expansion of the Benedictine Order that he founded exercised an enormous influence on the spread of Christianity throughout the European continent. He constitutes a fundamental point of reference for the unity of Europe and a powerful call to the irrefutable Christian roots of European culture and civilization."

The idea for this book first came to me during the evening of Pope Benedict's election. I had given a series of interviews for Independent Television News, and its 24-hour news channel. These live broadcasts were made from the television stands skilfully operated by the European Broadcasting Union, across the road from St Peter's Square, and on the roof of the *Urbaniana,* (Propaganda Fide). It was in the original college chapel of Propaganda Fide in Piazza di Spagna that Newman celebrated his first Mass as a Catholic priest on the Feast of Corpus Christi, 3 June 1847.

As Cardinal Ratzinger had strongly defended Catholic family values in his recent address at Subiaco, it seemed right to approach Family Publications with the idea and an outline for this book. An added attraction was the fact that this respected independent Catholic publishing house is based in Oxford, the city which had formed such an important part of Cardinal Newman's life from 1817 until his resignation from the position of Vicar of the University Church of St Mary the Virgin in 1843. The project was warmly welcomed by the publisher, Denis Riches, and his wife Valerie. Like Newman, they too are converts to Catholicism.

I remembered that Cardinal Ratzinger had described Newman as "the great English Cardinal, John Henry Newman", at a special Audience with Pope John Paul II for delegates attending a Newman Symposium, organised by the International Centre of Newman Friends, in Rome in April 1990. Introducing the delegates, Cardinal Ratzinger said: "Newman Scholars and Newman Friends from various countries, as well as professors and students from many Universities in Rome and elsewhere have met in these days in the Eternal City to celebrate in a fitting way the Centenary of the death of the great English Cardinal, John Henry Newman." He also mentioned how, as a seminarian, he was first introduced to the writings of Newman at the age of eighteen.

In welcoming John Paul II, he continued: "Holy Father, over the years of your pontificate you have repeatedly evoked the name of John Henry Newman as a spiritual father and inspiring master on the way to holiness and as a secure guide in the search for eternal truth."

Pope John Paul II began his address: "I welcome all of you and thank you for drawing attention through your celebration to the great English Cardinal's special place in the history of the Church. The passage of a hundred years since his death has done nothing to diminish the importance of this extraordinary figure, many of whose ideas enjoy a particular relevance in our own day."

Since I felt that there was no time to be lost I telephoned Fr Paul Chavasse, Provost of the Birmingham Oratory, and Postulator of the Newman Cause, and shared my initial ideas for this book. His response was most enthusiastic and he suggested that I could include previously unpublished pictures of Cardinal Newman from their archives. I also outlined my ideas to Archbishop Vincent Nichols of Birmingham, and he too was most supportive of the project. The following afternoon I visited the International Centre of Newman Friends run by the Spiritual Family The Work, situated on the Via Aurelia not far from Vatican City. There I talked with the Librarian, Sister Irene, who made several helpful suggestions.

Next I went to the Chiesa Nuova, the Rome Oratory, to the chapel of St Philip Neri, 1515-1595, Apostle of Rome, who founded the Congregation of the Oratory that Newman joined in 1846 following his ordination as a Catholic priest. Newman founded the English Congregation of the Oratory at Maryvale on the outskirts of Birmingham on 1 February 1848. I prayed that through the intercession of Our Lady and St Philip the book project would be blessed by the Most Holy Trinity.

The book includes a wide selection of letters, papers and sermons about Newman. Archbishop Vincent Nichols has written a chapter about Newman's Pastoral Work in Birmingham, which concludes with a thought-provoking reflection. Fr Paul Chavasse, Postulator of the Newman Cause, has contributed a history of the Cause for the Canonization of John Henry Newman. Cardinal Cormac Murphy-O'Connor, Archbishop of Westminster, has contributed a chapter on the Importance of Cardinal Newman Today. The Newman Centenary Year of 1990 was marked by a series of special events, and full texts of a number of particularly important sermons of that year have been included in the book. The volume would not be complete without a Benedictine contribution, which comes from the Abbot of Quarr Abbey, Dom Cuthbert Johnson OSB.

The *Decree on Heroic Virtues of the Servant of God John Henry Newman* was published on 22 January 1991. In it Pope John Paul II solemnly declared that: "It is certain that the Servant of God, John Henry Newman, Cardinal of the Holy Roman Church, Founder of the Oratory of St Philip Neri in England, had practised the theological virtues of Faith, Hope and Charity towards God and his neighbour, also the cardinal virtues of Prudence, Justice, Temperance and Fortitude and those connected with them, to a heroic degree, in accordance with the requirements of the investigation of this case."

The book highlights the personal interest that Popes from Leo XIII in the nineteenth century have taken in Newman, his teachings and the cause for his canonization. Pope Paul VI expressed interest in the Newman cause during the Holy Year of 1975, when Fr Stephen Dessain, the great Newman scholar from the Birmingham Oratory, presented him with three volumes of the *Letters and Diaries of John Henry Newman*.

In a letter to Archbishop Dwyer of Birmingham, Pope John Paul II wrote in 1979: "It is my hope that this centenary will be for all of us an opportunity for studying more closely the inspiring thought of Newman's genius, which speaks to us of deep intellectual honesty, fidelity to conscience and grace, piety and priestly zeal, devotion to Christ's Church and love of her doctrine, unconditional trust in divine providence and absolute obedience to the will of God."

Pope John Paul added: "I also wish to express my personal interest in the process for beatification of this "good and faithful servant" of Christ and the Church. I shall follow with close attention whatever progress may be made in this regard."

As recently as May 2005 Pope Benedict XVI, wrote about Cardinal Newman in a

Letter to Cardinal Jean-Marie Lustiger, Archbishop Emeritus of Paris. It was read in Trinity College chapel on Friday 13 May: "I was pleased to learn that you have been invited to offer Holy Mass at Trinity College, Oxford, as part of the celebrations marking the 450th anniversary of the establishment of that distinguished institution, which was the beloved *alma mater* of John Henry Cardinal Newman and which later elected him its first Honorary Fellow. It was at Trinity College that the young Newman learned those habits of mind and heart which guided him through a life of disciplined commitment to the pursuit of religious truth."

Will it be Benedict XVI, the first Pope of the twenty-first century, who will canonize John Henry Newman, and declare him a Doctor of the Church? Except for the martyrs, Newman would be the first English saint canonized since the Reformation.

Peter Jennings
Birmingham
11 August 2005

Part one

Newman

and

Benedict XVI

Pope Benedict XVI blessing the crowds in St Peter's Square following
his Inaugural Mass on Sunday, 24 April 2005.

Fotografia Felici

Biography of Benedict XVI

This is the official biography of Cardinal Joseph Ratzinger, contained in the booklet Sede Vacante 2005, *Biographical Notes of Cardinal Electors, prepared by the Holy See Press Office, in different languages. The booklet contained the biographical details of all 115 Cardinals participating in the Conclave that began in the Sistine Chapel on Monday 18 April 2005.*

CARDINAL JOSEPH RATZINGER, Prefect of the Congregation for the Doctrine of the Faith, President of the Pontifical Biblical Commission and International Theological Commission, Dean of the College of Cardinals, was born on 16 April 1927 in Marktl am Inn, Bavaria, Germany. He was ordained a priest on 29 June 1951.

His father, a police officer, came from a traditional family of farmers from Lower Bavaria. He spent his adolescent years in Traunstein, and was called into the auxiliary anti-aircraft service in the last months of World War II. From 1946 to 1951, the year in which he was ordained a priest and began to teach, he studied philosophy and theology at the University of Munich and at the seminary in Freising.

In 1953 he obtained a doctorate in theology with a thesis entitled: The People and House of God in St Augustine's doctrine of the Church. Four years later, he qualified as a university teacher. He then taught dogma and fundamental theology at the higher school of philosophy and theology of Freising, then in Bonn from 1959 to 1969, Münster from 1963 to 1966, Tübingen from 1966 to 1969. From 1969, he was a professor of dogmatic theology and of the history of dogma at the University of Regensburg and Vice President of the same university.

Already in 1962 he was well known when, at the age of 35, he became a consultor at Vatican Council II, of the Archbishop of Cologne, Cardinal Joseph Frings. Among his numerous publications, a particular place belongs to the *Introduction to Christianity,* a collection of university lectures on the profession of apostolic faith, published in 1968; and *Dogma and Revelation,* an anthology of essays, sermons and reflections dedicated to the pastoral ministry, published in 1973.

In March 1977, Paul VI selected him to be Archbishop of Munich and Freising and on 28 May 1977 he was consecrated, the first diocesan priest for 80 years to take over the pastoral ministry of this large Bavarian diocese.

He was created and proclaimed Cardinal priest by Paul VI in the consistory of 27 June 1977, and on 5 April 1993 he became Cardinal-Bishop, with the title of the Suburbicarian Church of Velletri-Segni (5 April 1993) and then, as senior Cardinal-Bishop and Dean of the Sacred College, to the Suburbicarian Church of Ostia (30 November 2002).

On 25 November 1981 he was nominated by John Paul II Prefect of the Congregation for the Doctrine of the Faith and President of the Biblical Commission and of the Pontifical International Theological Commission.

Relator of the 5th General Assembly of the Synod of Bishops (1980).

President Delegate to the 6th Synodal Assembly (1983).

Elected Vice Dean of the College of Cardinals, 6 November 1998.

On 30 November 2002, the Holy Father approved his election, by the order of cardinal bishops, as Dean of the College of Cardinals.

President of the Commission for the Preparation of the Catechism of the Catholic Church, and after 6 years of work (1986-92) he presented the New Catechism to the Holy Father.

Laurea honoris causa in jurisprudence from the Libera Università Maria Santissima Assunta, 10 November 1999.

Honorary member of the Pontifical Academy of Sciences, 13 November 2000.

Curial Membership:

Secretariat of State (second section)

Oriental Churches, Divine Worship and Discipline of the Sacraments, Bishops, Evangelization of Peoples, Catholic Education (congregations)

Christian Unity (council)

Latin America, Ecclesia Dei (commissions)

Cardinal Joseph Ratzinger was elected Pope on the fourth ballot during the afternoon of Tuesday, 19 April 2005. He chose the name Benedict XVI.

Cardinal John Henry Newman by Sir John Everett Millais, 1881.

Courtesy of the National Portrait Gallery, London

Manuscript of *Lead, kindly Light*

"Lead, kindly Light", or to give it Newman's title, "The Pillar of the Cloud", was written on 16 June 1833, while becalmed at sea, on board the *Count Ruggiero*, in the Straits of Bonifacio. Newman, who was travelling back from Sicily, where he had been seriously ill, to Marseilles, occupied his time writing verses. This poem, which has several musical settings, was first published in *Lyra Apostolica* (No 52).

Courtesy of the Fathers of the Birmingham Oratory

Chronology of the life of John Henry Newman

1801 - 1890

1801   21 February: Newman born at Old Broad Street, London, the eldest of six children.

9 April: Newman is baptised in the church of St Benet Fink, London.

1808   1 May: Enters Dr Nicholas' school at Ealing.

1816   8 March: His father's bank fails.

1 August - 21 December: Newman undergoes his "first Conversion".

14 December: Newman is matriculated at Trinity College, Oxford, as a commoner.

1817   8 June: Newman takes up residence at Trinity College, Oxford.

30 November: Newman's first communion in the Church of England, Trinity Chapel.

1818   18 May: Newman is elected a scholar of Trinity College.

1820   5 December: Newman takes his degree which was "below the line" – a third.

1821   1 November: Newman's father is declared bankrupt.

1822   11 January: Newman decides to take Orders in the Church of England.

12 April: Newman is elected a Fellow of Oriel College, Oxford.

1824   13 June: Newman is ordained deacon of the Church of England in Christ Church Cathedral, Oxford.

23 June: Newman preaches his first sermon at Over Worton, near Oxford.

4 July: Newman begins his pastoral ministry as curate in the parish of St Clement, Oxford.

29 September: Newman's father dies.

1825   26 March: Newman accepts position of Vice-Principal of Alban Hall, Oxford.

29 May, Whit Sunday: Newman is ordained a priest in the Church of England, Christ Church Cathedral, Oxford.

1826   21 February: Newman resigns as curate of St Clement's and Vice-Principal of Alban Hall on his appointment as a tutor of Oriel College.

2 July: Newman preaches his first University Sermon.

1828   2 February: Newman is appointed Vicar of the University Church of St Mary the Virgin, Oxford.

23 June: Newman begins a systematic reading of the Fathers of the Church.

1831   June: Newman begins work on the *Arians of the Fourth Century*.

1832   31 July: Newman finishes work on the *Arians of the Fourth Century*.

3 December: Newman sets out on journey to the Mediterranean with H Froude and his father.

1833 April-May: The Froudes having departed for England, Newman returns to Sicily alone and contracts a severe fever.

16 June: On the ship from Palermo to Marseilles Newman writes the poem *Lead, kindly Light.*

9 July: Newman arrives back in England.

14 July: Keble preaches the Assize Sermon in St Mary's Church, Oxford, on 'National Apostasy' which Newman considers the beginning of the Oxford Movement.

9 September: Newman publishes the first of the *Tracts for the Times.*

5 November: *The Arians of the Fourth Century* is published.

1834 30 June: Newman begins daily service at St Mary's, Oxford.

1835 27 March: Volume Two of the *Parochial Sermons* is published.

1836 29 January: Volume Three of the *Parochial Sermons* is published.

17 May: Newman's mother dies.

22 September: Dedication of the new church at Littlemore.

1838 30 March: *Lectures on Justification* is published.

30 November: Volume Four of the *Parochial Sermons* is published.

1839 July-September: Newman's first doubts about the position of the Anglican Church.

1840 Volume Five of the *Parochial Sermons* is published.

1841 27 February: *Tract 90* is published.

July – September: Recurrence of doubts about the position of the Anglican Church.

1842 February: Volume Six of the *Parochial Sermons* is published.

19 April: Newman goes to live at Littlemore.

1843 18 September: Newman resigns the benefice of St Mary's Church, Oxford.

25 September: Newman preaches his last sermon as an Anglican, 'The Parting of Friends', in the church at Littlemore.

1845 9 October: Newman is received into the Catholic Church at Littlemore by Fr (now Blessed) Dominic Barberi, the Italian Passionist (beatified by Pope Paul VI on 27 October 1963).

10 October: Newman receives his First Holy Communion in the Catholic Church.

1 November: Newman confirmed at New College Oscott, by Bishop Wiseman.

1846 23 February: Newman leaves Littlemore for Old Oscott, renamed "Mary's Vale" - Maryvale.

7 September: Newman sets off with Ambrose St John to Rome for studies at Propaganda.

1847 21 February: Pope Pius IX approves Newman's decision to start an Oratory in England.

30 May: Trinity Sunday: Newman is ordained priest in Rome by Cardinal Franzoni.

27 November: Newman receives brief for the foundation of the Oratory.

31 December: Newman arrives back at Maryvale.

1848   1 February: English Congregation of the Oratory is set up at Maryvale.

14 February: Newman admits Fr Faber into the Oratory.

Newman moves to St Wilfrid's, Cotton, having given up Maryvale.

1849   2 February: Oratory opens at Alcester Street, Birmingham.

15 April: Oratory divided into two – Newman remains in Birmingham and Faber moves to London.

15 September: Newman goes to Bilston to relieve parish priest during a cholera epidemic.

November: *Discourses to Mixed Congregations* is published.

1850   May–June: Newman gives 'Lectures on Certain difficulties felt by Anglicans in submitting to the Catholic Church' at the London Oratory.

22 August: Newman receives honorary degree of Doctor of Divinity conferred by Pope Pius IX.

29 September: The English Hierarchy is restored by Pope Pius IX.

1851   June: Newman begins *Lectures on the Present Position of Catholics*, delivered in the old Corn Exchange, Birmingham.

8 July: Newman denounces the apostate priest Achilli.

30 September: Newman visits Ireland for the first time.

4 November: Newman is indicted for libel by Achilli.

12 November: Newman is appointed Rector of the proposed Catholic University of Ireland.

1852   16 February: Oratory moves to new house in Edgbaston.

10 May – 7 June: In Dublin Newman delivers first five of his Discourses on the Scope and Nature of University education.

21-24 June: The Achilli trial in which the jury decides that Newman has not proved his charges.

13 July: Newman preaches *The Second Spring* at the First Synod of the New Province of Westminster, held at Oscott College.

1853   31 January: Newman loses libel case and is fined £100.

August: *Verses on Religious Subjects* is published in Dublin.

17 October – 3 November: Newman gives Lectures *The History of the Turks* in Liverpool, published in 1854.

22 November: Opening of the temporary Church of the Oratory, in Edgbaston.

1854   4 June: Newman is installed as Rector of the Catholic University in Dublin, and begins the *Catholic University Gazette*.

3 November: Official opening of the Catholic University.

1855   October – November: Dispute between Birmingham and London Oratories.

1856   12 January: Newman and St John arrive in Rome, having visited Oratories en route.

1 May: Newman's University Church is opened in Dublin.

Callista, a novel, a sketch of the third century, is published.

1857   3 April: Newman announces to the Irish bishops his intention of resigning the Rectorship of the Catholic University.

27 August: Newman receives request from Cardinal Wiseman on behalf of the Hierarchy to undertake the supervision of a new translation of the Scriptures into English.

Sermons Preached on Various Occasions is published.

1858   12 November: Newman formally resigns the Rectorship of the Catholic University of Ireland.

1859   21 March: Newman agrees to become editor of *The Rambler* magazine.

2 May: Oratory School is opened in Edgbaston.

22 May: Bishop Ullathorne asks Newman to give up editorship of *The Rambler*.

July: Newman publishes his article, 'On Consulting the Faithful in Matters of Doctrine', which is delated to Rome for heresy by Bishop Brown of Newport.

1863   30 December: Newman receives Macmillan's Magazine for January 1864 containing Kingsley's attack.

1864   12 February: Newman publishes correspondence with Kingsley arising out of the attack.

20 March: Kingsley replies with pamphlet: *What then does Dr Newman mean?*

21 April – 2 June: Newman publishes a history of his religious opinions in seven weekly parts entitled: *Apologia pro vita sua*.

24 October: Newman buys land in Oxford and prepares to build a church, having been offered the Catholic Mission there by Bishop Ullathorne.

December: Newman sells land in Oxford in view of Propaganda's opposition to Catholics going to Protestant Universities.

1865   May-June: Newman's poem, 'The Dream of Gerontius', is published in *The Month*.

1866   31 January: Newman publishes *A Letter to the Rev E B Pusey, concerning the Doctrine of Mary*.

8 June: Newman accedes to Bishop Ullathorne's request that he takes up the Oxford Mission, and that he sets up an Oratory there.

1867   Newman makes a second attempt to set up the Oxford mission and a proposed new Oratory.

1868   4 January: *Verses on Various Occasions* is published.

16 June: Newman and St John visit Littlemore for the first time since 1846.

1870   15 March: *An Essay in Aid of a Grammar of Assent* is published.

October: *Essays on Miracles* is published.

1875   14 January: *A Letter to the Duke of Norfolk* is published.

24 May: Newman's closest friend and companion, Ambrose St John, dies.

1877   14 December: Newman is invited to become the first Honorary Fellow of Trinity College, Oxford.

1878   26-28 February: Newman visits Oxford for the first time since 1846, staying at Trinity College.

1879   31 January: Newman receives news that he is to be made a Cardinal.

18 March: Newman receives official word from the Cardinal Secretary of State, announcing he is to receive the Cardinalate.

12 May: Newman delivers his 'Biglietto speech' in Rome.

15 May: Newman receives the Cardinal's hat at a public consistory and is created Cardinal Deacon of San Giorgio in Velabro by Pope Leo XIII.

1 July: Newman is welcomed at the Oratory church, on his arrival back in Birmingham.

1880   8-15 May: Newman is guest of the Duke of Norfolk in London where receptions and dinners are held in his honour.

22-25 May: Newman visits Trinity College, Oxford, and preaches morning and evening in St Aloysius's church, 23 May.

1881   25 June – 6 July: Newman stays at London Oratory and preaches, 26 June.

1886   October: Newman has a fall and receives the anointing of the sick. He recovers.

1889   November: Newman calls on George Cadbury about compulsory attendance of Catholic girl employees at daily prayer meeting.

25 December, Christmas Day: Newman says Mass for the last time.

1890   10 August: Newman receives the Last Sacraments.

11 August: 8.45 pm Newman dies of pneumonia in his room at The Oratory House in Edgbaston.

19 August: Funeral Mass. Newman is buried in the Oratorian cemetery at Rednal, near Birmingham.

1991   22 January: Decree on Heroic Virtues is signed by Pope John Paul II. Newman is declared Venerable.

John Henry Newman from a miniature by Sir William Ross c. 1845.

Courtesy of the Fathers of the Birmingham Oratory

Benedict XVI explains
why he chose the name of Benedict

First General Audience, Wednesday 27 April 2005

In his first general audience, which was held on Wednesday 27 April 2005, in St. Peter's Square in the presence of 15,000 people, Pope Benedict again gave thanks to God for having been elected as Peter's successor, and explained why he chose the name of Benedict.

The Pope said: "I wish to speak of the name I chose on becoming Bishop of Rome and pastor of the universal Church. I chose to call myself Benedict XVI ideally as a link to the venerated Pontiff, Benedict XV, who guided the Church through the turbulent times of the First World War. He was a true and courageous prophet of peace who struggled strenuously and bravely, first to avoid the drama of war and then to limit its terrible consequences.

"In his footsteps I place my ministry, in the service of reconciliation and harmony between peoples, profoundly convinced that the great good of peace is above all a gift of God, a fragile and precious gift to be invoked, safeguarded and constructed, day after day and with everyone's contribution.

"The name Benedict also evokes the extraordinary figure of the great 'patriarch of western monasticism', St Benedict of Nursia, co-patron of Europe with Cyril and Methodius. The progressive expansion of the Benedictine Order which he founded exercised an enormous influence on the spread of Christianity throughout the European continent. For this reason, St Benedict is much venerated in Germany, and especially in Bavaria, my own land of origin; he constitutes a fundamental point of reference for the unity of Europe and a powerful call to the irrefutable Christian roots of European culture and civilization."

The Pope appealed to St Benedict for help "to hold firm Christ's central position in our lives. May he always be first in our thoughts and in all our activities!"

Before concluding, Pope Benedict XVI announced that, just as at the beginning of his pontificate John Paul II had continued the reflections on Christian virtues begun by Pope John Paul I, in future weekly audiences he would resume the comments prepared by John Paul II on the second part of the Psalms and Canticles, which are part of Vespers. "From next Wednesday, I will begin precisely from where his catechesis was interrupted after the general audience of 26 January."

John Henry Newman 1863, photographed by Robert Thrupp.

Courtesy of the Fathers of the Birmingham Oratory

Part two

"John Henry Newman – Lover of Truth"

Academic Newman Symposium

Rome, April 1990

Organised by

The International Centre of Newman Friends

(Rome; Littlemore, Oxford; Bregenz, Austria; Jerusalem)

Pope John Paul II with Cardinal Joseph Ratzinger, Archbishop (later Cardinal) Edward Cassidy (left), Bishop Klaus Küng of Feldkirch (right) and delegates at the International Newman Symposium during the Papal Audience on 27 April 1990.

L'Osservatore Romano

Cardinal Joseph Ratzinger's words of greeting

to Pope John Paul II

27 April 1990

Your Holiness,

Newman Scholars and Newman Friends from various countries, as well as professors and students from many Universities in Rome and elsewhere have met in these days in the Eternal City to celebrate in a fitting way the Centenary of the death of the great English Cardinal, John Henry Newman. May I, on behalf of them all, Holy Father, express our deep joy and our gratitude for this special audience which you have granted to the participants in these Celebrations.

Holy Father,
Over the years of your pontificate you have repeatedly evoked the name of John Henry Newman as a spiritual father and inspiring master on the way to holiness and as a secure guide in the search for eternal truth. In a letter addressed to the then Archbishop of Birmingham, His Grace George Patrick Dwyer, you wrote in 1979: "It is my hope that the centenary of his Cardinalate will be for all of us an opportunity for studying more closely the inspiring thought of Newman's genius, which speaks to us of deep intellectual honesty, fidelity to conscience and grace, piety and priestly zeal, devotion to Christ's Church and love of her doctrine, unconditional trust in divine providence and absolute obedience to the will of God."

During your pastoral visit to Great Britain in 1982 you again pronounced very significant words concerning Cardinal Newman: "I cannot come to the Midlands without remembering that great man of God, that pilgrim for truth, Cardinal John Henry Newman. His quest for God and for the fullness of truth − a sign of the Holy Spirit at work within him − brought him to a prayerfulness and a wisdom which still inspire us today …." (Homily at Coventry, *L'Osservatore Romano*, 31 May 1982).

This Symposium, sponsored by the International Community The Work with its Newman Centres in Rome, Bregenz in Austria, Littlemore near Oxford and in Jerusalem, has been made possible by the generosity of noble-hearted benefactors, among whom we gratefully wish to mention several Bishops of German dioceses.

A highlight of this Symposium, in the spirit of Cardinal Newman, was the valued visit of the honorable President of Italy, Francesco Cossiga, who is not only a Newman Friend but figures among Newman scholars. Furthermore it is gratifying to see the great interest in Newman's life and work not only among scholars and friends of the Cardinal, but also among members of the Hierarchy.

It is a special joy for us that among those who contributed in various ways to this Symposium, there were representatives of the Anglican Church, and that the Archbishop of Canterbury, Robert Runcie, has sent a message. May Cardinal Newman, whose love of truth was so deep and pure, remain a bridge between the various denominations and continue to inspire us to serve unity in a spirit of charity (cf. Ephesians 4:15).

Holy Father, all of us who are gathered here, promise to take to heart the words which you addressed in 1979 to pilgrims from the Archdiocese of Birmingham: "May you and the whole Church draw inspiration from Newman's sincere faith and holy life," as well as the message you may wish to give us today.

With this intention in mind we ask your Apostolic Blessing for the participants of our Symposium, for the members of the Birmingham Oratory, for the members of the International Community of The Work, for all who work towards Newman's beatification, for all Newman scholars and Newman friends all over the world, as well as for the many who turn with trust and confidence to this great English Cardinal.

Pope John Paul II greeting Cardinal Joseph Ratzinger.

L'Osservatore Romano

Address given by Pope John Paul II

27 April 1990

Your Eminences, Excellencies, My Brothers and Sisters in Christ,

I am very pleased that this meeting allows me to take part as it were in the Academic Symposium which the International Community 'The Work' and the Centre of Newman Friends have organized to commemorate the centenary of the death of the renowned Cardinal John Henry Newman. I welcome all of you and thank you for drawing attention through your celebration to the great English Cardinal's special place in the history of the Church. The passage of a hundred years since his death has done nothing to diminish the importance of this extraordinary figure, many of whose ideas enjoy a particular relevance in our own day. The theme of your Symposium, 'John Henry Newman - Lover of Truth', points to a major reason for the continuing attraction of Newman's life and writings. His was a lifelong pursuit of the Truth which alone can make men free (cf. John 8:32).

In this brief encounter I can mention only some of the many lessons which Newman holds out to the Church and to the world of culture. I would underline the inspiration that scholars and thoughtful readers of Newman continue to receive today from this pilgrim for truth. Your Symposium and other such celebrations during this centenary year offer the occasion for a deeper appreciation of Newman's charism. Not least, he reminds us of the need for an interior disposition of loving obedience to God if contemporary society is to be successful in its quest for the full liberating truth which it urgently needs, and indeed knows itself to need.

Ever since his first conversion grace at the age of fifteen, Newman was never to lose his sense of God's presence, his respect for revealed truth and his thirst for holiness of life. In his own lifetime, the example of his singular piety and integrity was widely esteemed throughout England by both Catholics and Anglicans alike. His reputation as a man of deep spirituality as well as of learning was one of the principal motives inspiring the English laity to petition Pope Leo XIII to raise the founder of the English Oratory to the College of Cardinals (cf. *Letters and Diaries of John Henry Newman* XXIX, Oxford, 1976 p. 85).

Newman's intellectual and spiritual pilgrimage was made in earnest response to an inner light of which he seemed always aware, the light which conscience projects on all of life's movements and endeavours. For Newman, conscience was a messenger from Him who, both in nature and in grace, speaks to us behind a veil (*Difficulties of Anglicans* II, Westminster, Md., p. 248). It inevitably led him to obedience to the authority of the Church, first in the Anglican Communion, and later as a Catholic. His preaching and writings reflected his own lived experience. So, he could instruct his listeners: "Do but examine your thoughts and doings; do but attempt what you know to be God's will, and you will most assuredly be led on into all the truth: you will recognize the force, meaning and awful graciousness of the Gospel Creed ..." (*Parochial and Plain Sermons* VIII, p. 120). Newman did not seek worldly success for his own sake, nor did he let the misunderstanding which often accompanied his efforts distract him from the search for true holiness, which was always his conscious aim. He enjoyed great influence and authority during his life, not for any office that he held but because of the human and spiritual personality which he portrayed.

The inner drama which marked his long life hinged on the question of holiness and union with Christ. His over-riding desire was to know and to do God's will. Thus at a time of intense spiritual questioning, before retiring to pray about his decision to enter the Catholic Church, he asked his parishioners at Littlemore to "remember such a one in time to come, though you hear him not, and pray for him, that in all things he may know God's will, and at all times he may be ready to fulfil it." (*Sermons bearing on Subjects of the Day,* Westminster, Md., 1968, p. 409).

This ideal sustained him in the difficult hour when he sacrificed so much in leaving his beloved and familiar Church of England in order to enter the Catholic Church. His reasoned fidelity to the way God's Providence led him, made this experience – what he called the "hidden years" of his life – a source of encouragement and inspiration for many who were looking for the "port after a rough sea" (*Apologia pro vita sua,* London, 1888, p. 238). With letters of spiritual direction and counsel he helped countless others along the path of the truth he himself had found and which filled him with so much joy. Newman's influence in this sense has increased over the past hundred years and is no longer limited to England. All over the world people claim that this master of the spirit by his works, by his example, by his intercession, has been an instrument of divine providence in their lives.

In the contemporary cultural climate, with particular reference to Europe, there is an area of Newman's thought which deserves special attention. I refer to the unity which he advocated between theology and science, between the world of faith and the world of reason. He proposed that learning should not lack unity, but be rooted in a total view. Thus he concluded his discourses before the University of Dublin with these striking words: "I wish the intellect to range with the utmost freedom, and religion to enjoy an equal freedom but what I am stipulating for is, that they should be found in one and the same place, and exemplified in the same persons." (*Sermons preached on various occasions,* London, 1904, p. 13).

In the present changing circumstances of European culture, does Newman not indicate the essential Christian contribution to building a new era based on a deeper truth and higher values? He wrote: "I want to destroy that diversity of centres, which puts everything into confusion by creating a contrariety of influences. I wish the same spots and the same individuals to be at once oracles of philosophy and shrines of devotion ..." (ibid.). In this endeavour the path the Church must follow is succinctly expressed by the English Cardinal in this way: "The Church fears no knowledge, but she purifies all; she represses no element of our nature, but cultivates the whole." (*The Idea of a University,* Westminster, Md, p. 234).

Still another area of Newman's spiritual itinerary stands out as particularly relevant in the wake of the Second Vatican Council. Because of it we feel Newman to be our true spiritual contemporary. The mystery of the Church always remained the great love of John Henry Newman's life. And in this there is a further profound lesson for the present.

Newman's writings project an eminently clear picture of his unwavering love of the Church as the continuing outpouring of God's love for man in every phase of history. His was a truly spiritual vision, capable of perceiving all the weaknesses present in the human fabric of the Church, but equally sure in its perception of the mystery hidden beyond our material gaze. May his memory inspire us to make our own the significant prayer that flowed so naturally from his heart: "Let me never forget that thou hast established on earth a kingdom of thy own, that the Church is thy work, Thy establishment, thy instrument; that we are under thy rule, thy laws and thy eye — that when the Church speaks thou dost speak. Let not familiarity with this wonderful truth lead me to be insensible to it — let not the weakness of thy human representatives lead me to forget that it is thou who dost speak and act through them." (*Meditations and Devotions,* Westminster, Md., pp. 378-379).

May these same sentiments fill all our hearts as we commemorate this eminent churchman. In Newman's entire experience we hear the echo of the words of Jesus to Nicodemus: "He who does what is true comes to the light, that it may be clearly seen that his deeds have been wrought in God." (John 3:21). I trust that your Symposium will inspire further studies to bring out more clearly the importance and relevance of this "Lover of Truth" for our times. Upon you and Newman scholars and friends everywhere I invoke the light of the Holy Spirit so that through your efforts the teachings of this great English Cardinal may be better known and appreciated. I gladly impart my Apostolic Blessing.

Fr Vincent Blehl S J (left), with Cardinal Joseph Ratzinger, and Fr Paul Chavasse, during the Academic Symposium, "John Henry Newman – Lover of Truth" held in the Sala Borromini at the Chiesa Nuova, 26-28 April 1990, to celebrate the Centenary of the death of John Henry Newman.

L'Osservatore Romano

Newman belongs to the great teachers
of the Church

Cardinal Joseph Ratzinger

Introductory words for the third day of the Newman Symposium in Rome

Today's third and final day of our Newman Symposium is devoted to the echo that Newman's figure and work found, first at that time – one hundred years ago – and then, in the theology of the present time. I do not feel competent to speak on one or the other, but perhaps it is meaningful and in accord with the theme of this day, if I tell a little about my own way to Newman, in which indeed something is reflected of the presence of this great English theologian in the intellectual and spiritual struggle of our time.

In January 1946, when I began my study of theology in the Seminary in Freising which had finally reopened after the problems of the war, an older student was assigned as prefect to our group. Alfred Läpple had begun to work on a dissertation on Newman's theology of conscience even before the beginning of the war. In all the years of his military service he had not lost sight of this theme, which he now turned to with new enthusiasm and energy. Soon we were bonded by a personal friendship, wholly centred on the great problems of philosophy and theology. Newman was always present to us. He published his dissertation in 1952 with the title: *Der einzelne in der Kirche* (The Individual in the Church). Unfortunately the second volume which had been announced in it has still not been printed.

For us at that time, Newman's teaching on conscience became an important foundation for theological personalism, which was drawing us all in its sway. Our image of the human being as well as our image of the Church was permeated by this point of departure. We had experienced the claim of a totalitarian party, which understood itself as the fulfilment of history and which negated the conscience of the individual. One of its leaders had said: "I have no conscience. My conscience is Adolf Hitler." [1] The appalling devastation of humanity that followed was before our eyes. So it was liberating and essential for us to know that the "we" of the Church does not rest on a cancellation of conscience, but that, exactly the opposite, it can only develop from conscience. Precisely because Newman interpreted the existence of the human being from conscience, that is, from the relationship between God and the soul, it was clear that this personalism is not individualism, and that being bound by conscience does not mean being free to make random choices – the exact opposite is the case. It was from Newman that we learned to understand the primacy of the Pope. Freedom of conscience – Newman told us – is not

---

[1] A statement from Hermann Göring, cited in Th. Schieder, Hermann Rauschning *Gespräche mit Hitler* as historical source (Opladen, 1972) p. 19, note 25.

identical with the right "to dispense with conscience, to ignore a lawgiver and judge, to be independent of unseen obligations." Thus conscience in its true sense is the bedrock of papal authority. For its power comes from revelation that completes natural conscience, which is imperfectly enlightened, and "the championship of the Moral Law and of conscience is [the Pope's] *raison d'être.*"[2]

I hardly need to mention that this teaching on conscience has become ever more important for me in the continued development of the Church and the world. Ever more I see how it first opens in the context of the biography of the Cardinal, which is only to be understood in connection with the drama of his century and so speaks to us. Newman had become a convert as a man of conscience; it was his conscience that led him out of the old ties and securities into the world of Catholicism, which was difficult and strange for him. But this way of conscience is everything other than a way of self-sufficient subjectivity: it is a way of obedience to objective truth. The second step in Newman's lifelong journey of conversion was overcoming the subjective evangelical position in favour of an understanding of Christendom based on the objectivity of dogma.[3] In this respect I find a formulation from one of his early sermons to be still highly significant especially today: True Christendom is shown ... in obedience and not through a state of consciousness. "Thus the whole duty and work of a Christian is made up of these two parts, Faith and Obedience: 'looking unto Jesus' (Heb: 2,9) ... and acting according to his will ... I conceive that we are in danger, in this day, of insisting on neither of these as we ought; regarding all true and careful consideration of the Object of Faith, as barren orthodoxy, technical subtlety ... and ... making the test of our being religious, to consist in our having what is called a spiritual state of heart..."[4]. In this context some sentences from *The Arians of the Fourth Century* that sound rather astonishing at first seem important to me. "... to detect and to approve the principle on which ... peace is grounded in Scripture; to submit to the dictation of truth, as such, as a primary authority in matters of political and private conduct; to understand ... zeal to be prior in the succession of Christian graces to benevolence.[5] For me it is always fascinating to see and consider how in just this way and only in this way, through commitment to the truth, to God, conscience receives its rank, dignity and strength. I would like in this context to add but one sentence from the *Apologia*, which shows the realism in this idea of person and Church: "Living movements do not come of committees."[6]

Very briefly I would like to return to the autobiographical thread. When I continued my studies in Munich in 1947, I found a well-read and enthusiastic follower of Newman in the Fundamental Theologian, Gottlieb Söhngen, who was my true teacher in theology. He opened up *The Grammar of Assent* to us and in doing so, the special manner and form of certainty in religious knowledge. Even deeper for me was the contribution which Heinrich Fries published in connection with the Jubilee of Chalcedon. Here I found access to Newman's teaching on the development of doctrine, which I regard along with his

---

2 *Difficulties felt by Anglicans in Catholic Teaching II*, pp. 250, 253.
3 Cf. the careful presentation of this way by C S Dessain, *John Henry Newman. Anwalt redlichen Glaubens* (Freiburg, 1980); cf. also G Biemer, *J H Newman, 1801 – 1890, Leben und Werk* (Mainz, 1989).
4 *Parochial and Plain Sermons II*, p. 153f; cf. Dessain, p. 82.
5 *The Arians of the Fourth Century* p. 244; Dessain, p. 70.
6 *Apologia pro vita sua*, p. 39.

doctrine on conscience as his decisive contribution to the renewal of theology.[7] With this he had placed the key in our hand to build historical thought into theology or, much more, he taught us to think historically in theology and so to recognize the identity of faith in all developments. Here I have to refrain from deepening these ideas further. It seems to me that in modern theology Newman's starting point has not yet been fully evaluated. Fruitful possibilities awaiting development are still hidden in it. At this point I would only like to refer again to the biographical background of this concept. It is known how Newman's insight into the ideas of development influenced his way to Catholicism. But it is not just a matter of an unfolding of ideas. In the concept of development Newman's own life plays a role. That seems to become visible to me in his well known words: "…to live is to change, and to be perfect is to have changed often."[8] Throughout his entire life, Newman was a person converting, a person being transformed, and thus he always remained and became ever more himself.

Here the figure of St Augustine comes to my mind, with whom Newman was so associated. When Augustine was converted in the garden at Cassiciacum he understood conversion according to the system of the revered master Plotinus and the Neo-Platonic philosophers. He thought that his past sinful life would now be definitively cast off; from now on the convert would be someone wholly new and different and his further journey would be a steady climb to the ever purer heights of closeness to God. It was something like that which Gregory of Nyssa described in his *Ascent of Moses*: "Just as bodies, after having received the first push downwards, fall effortlessly into the depths with ever greater speed, so, on the contrary, the soul which has loosed itself from earthly passion rises up in a rapid upward movement … constantly overcoming itself in a steady upward flight."[9] Augustine's actual experience was a different one. He had to learn that being a Christian is always a difficult journey with all its heights and depths. The image of *ascensus* (ascent) is exchanged for that of *iter* (journey) whose tiring weight is lightened and borne up by moments of light, which we may receive now and then. Conversion is the *iter* − the roadway of a whole lifetime.[10] And faith is always 'development', and precisely in this manner it is the maturation of the soul to truth, to God, who is more intimate to us than we are to ourselves. In the idea of 'development' Newman had written his own experience of a never finished conversion and interpreted for us, not only the way of Christian doctrine, but that of the Christian life. The characteristic of the great doctor of the Church, it seems to me, is that he teaches not only through his thought and speech, but rather by his life, because within him thought and life are interpenetrated and defined. If this is so, then Newman belongs to the great teachers of the Church, because at the same time he touches our hearts and enlightens our thinking.

---

[7] H. Fries, *Die Dogmengeschichte des fünften Jahrhunderts im theologischen Werdegang von J H Newman*. In A Grillmeier (H Bacht (ed.)) *Das Konzil von Chalkedon Vol. III, Chalkedon heute* (Würzburg, 1954), pp. 421–454.

[8] *An Essay on the Development of Christian Doctrine* p. 40; cf. Dessain, p. 166.

[9] Gregory of Nyssa, *De vita Moysis* PG 44, p. 401A.

[10] Cf. the excellent description of the inner journey of Augustine from his return to Africa until his consecration as bishop in P Brown, *Augustinus von Hippo*. Translated from the English by J Bernard, (Leipzig, 1972), pp. 126–136, especially p. 132.

John Henry Newman, photograph by Heath and Beau, London, December 1861. This was the first official photograph taken of Dr. Newman.

Courtesy of the Fathers of the Birmingham Oratory

Message from the
Archbishop of Canterbury

*Dr Robert Runcie sent the following message
from Lambeth Palace, London, during April 1990,
to the Newman Symposium in Rome*

It gives me great pleasure to greet you as you begin your celebrations of the life of John Henry Newman, in this the centenary year of his death. I have already offered a small contribution to our parallel celebrations here in Britain. Newman occupies a unique place in the history of both our traditions. As an Anglican he reminded us of our roots in the Fathers and of our faith within Catholic Christendom. As a Catholic he helped towards a better understanding of the history of dogma and prepared for the great developments this century in the Second Vatican Council.

Your programme identifies themes that would have been close to Newman's heart. His evangelical roots meant that he always took revelation seriously. His journey to Roman Catholicism was partly inspired by his search for the true authority of the Church. Finally, I am encouraged to see that you will be looking at Newman's influence, both at the time of his death and in our contemporary world. Newman still has much to teach us. Perhaps his most essential contribution is to remind us to treasure the tradition but at the same time to take seriously the culture within which we live. These are lessons from which in different ways both our Churches can still learn.

The climate of thought has changed greatly in this past century. I am able to write to you now as my predecessor could not in 1890, for now we share a sense of communion, which was not shared then. Newman's journey and his intellectual example should encourage us never to rest complacently. He challenges us to look further ahead along the road. May his part in our two traditions support us, as we work still for that full communion for which we know Christ prayed. I wish you well in your Celebrations and trust that they will assist us to move on together on our common journey of faith.

The contributions in this section are published in: *John Henry Newman, Lover of Truth: Academic Symposium and Celebration of the First Centenary of the Death of John Henry Newman,* ed. Strolz/Binder, International Centre of Newman Friends, Rome, Urbaniana University Press, 1991, pp. 137–139, 7–11, 141–146, 157f.

Fr John Henry Newman in his Oratorian habit, by
Heath and Beau, December 1861.

Courtesy of the Fathers of the Birmingham Oratory

Part three

Ratzinger on Newman:

Conscience and Truth

Cardinal Joseph Ratzinger, Prefect of the Congregation for the Doctrine of the Faith, signing the visitors book during the Academic Symposium, "John Henry Newman – Lover of Truth" held in the Sala Borromini and the Chiesa Nuova, Rome, 26-28 April 1990, to celebrate the Centenary of the Death of John Henry Newman.

L'Osservatore Romano

Conscience and Truth

Cardinal Joseph Ratzinger

Presented at the tenth Workshop for Bishops
February 1991, Dallas, Texas, USA

In the contemporary discussion on what constitutes the essence of morality and how it can be recognized, the question of conscience has become paramount especially in the field of Catholic moral theology. This discussion centres on the concepts of freedom and norm, autonomy and heteronomy, self-determination and external determination by authority. Conscience appears here as the bulwark of freedom in contrast to the encroachments of authority on existence. In the course of this, two notions of the Catholic are set in opposition to each other. One is a renewed understanding of the Catholic essence which expounds Christian faith from the basis of freedom and as the very principle of freedom itself. The other is a superseded, "pre-conciliar" model which subjects Christian existence to authority, regulating life even into its most intimate preserves, and thereby attempts to maintain control over people's lives. Morality of conscience and morality of authority, as two opposing models, appear to be locked in a struggle with each other. Accordingly, the freedom of the Christian would be rescued by appeal to the classical principle of moral tradition that conscience is the highest norm which man is to follow, even in opposition to authority. Authority in this case, the Magisterium, may well speak of matters moral, but only in the sense of presenting conscience with material for its own deliberation. Conscience would retain, however, the final word. Some authors reduce conscience in its aspect of final arbiter to the formula: conscience is infallible.

Nonetheless, at this point, a contradiction can arise. It is of course undisputed that one must follow a certain conscience or at least not act against it. But whether the judgment of conscience, or what one takes to be such, is always right, indeed whether it is infallible, is another question. For if this were the case, it would mean that there is no truth — at least not in moral and religious matters, which is to say, in the areas which constitute the very pillars of our existence. For judgments of conscience can contradict each other. Thus there could be at best the subject's own truth, which would be reduced to the subject's sincerity. No door or window would lead from the subject into the broader world of being and human solidarity. Whoever thinks this through will come to the realization that no real freedom exists then and that the supposed pronouncements of conscience are but the reflection of social circumstances. This should necessarily lead to the conclusion that placing freedom in opposition to authority overlooks something. There must be something deeper if freedom, and therefore human existence, are to have meaning.

1. A Conversation on the Erroneous Conscience and first Inferences

It has become apparent that the question of conscience leads in fact to the core of the moral problem and thus to the question of man's existence itself. I would now like to pursue this question not in the form of a strictly conceptual and therefore unavoidably abstract presentation, but by way of narrative, as one might say today, by relating, to begin with, the story of my own encounter with this problem. I first became aware of the question with all its urgency in the beginning of my academic teaching. In the course of a dispute, a senior colleague, who was keenly aware of the problems of being Christian in our times, expressed the opinion that one should actually be grateful to God that He allows there to be so many unbelievers in good conscience. For if their eyes were opened and they became believers, they would not be capable, in this world of ours, of bearing the burden of faith with all its moral obligations. But as it is, since they can go another way in good conscience, they can reach salvation. What shocked me about this assertion was not in the first place the idea of an erroneous conscience given by God Himself in order to save men by means of such artfulness – the idea, so to speak, of a blindness sent by God for the salvation of those in question. What disturbed me was the notion that it harbored, that faith is a burden which can hardly be borne and which no doubt was intended only for stronger natures – faith almost as a kind of punishment, in any case an imposition not easily coped with. According to this view, faith would not make salvation easier but harder. Being happy would mean not being burdened with having to believe or having to submit to the moral yoke of the faith of the Catholic Church. The erroneous conscience, which makes life easier and marks a more human course, would then be a real grace, the normal way to salvation. Untruth, keeping truth at bay, would be better for man than truth. It would not be the truth that would set him free, but rather he would have to be freed from the truth. Man would be more at home in the dark than in the light. Faith would not be the good gift of the good God but instead an affliction. If this were the state of affairs, how could faith give rise to joy? Who would have the courage to pass faith on to others? Would it not be better to spare them the truth or even keep them from it? In the last few decades, notions of this sort have discernibly crippled the disposition to evangelize. The one who sees the faith as a heavy burden or as a moral imposition is unable to invite others to believe. Rather he lets them be, in the putative freedom of their good consciences.

The one who spoke in this manner was a sincere believer and, I would say, a strict Catholic who performed his moral duty with care and conviction. But he expressed a form of experience of faith which is disquieting. Its propagation could only be fatal to the faith. The almost traumatic aversion many have to what they hold to be 'pre-conciliar' Catholicism is rooted, I am convinced, in the encounter with such a faith seen only as encumbrance. Certainly, some very basic questions arise. Can such a faith actually be an encounter with truth? Is the truth about God and man so sad and difficult, or does truth not lie in the overcoming of such legalism? Does it not lie in freedom? But where does freedom lead? What course does it chart for us? At the conclusion, we shall come back to these fundamental problems of Christian existence today, but before we do that we must return to the core of our topic, namely, the matter of conscience. What unsettled me in the argument just recounted was first of all the caricature of faith I perceived in it. In a second course of reflection, it occurred to me further that the concept of conscience which it implied must also be wrong. The erroneous conscience, by sheltering the person from the exacting demands of truth, saves him − thus went the argument. Conscience does not appear here as a window through which one can see outward to that common truth which builds and sustains us all, and so makes possible, through the common recognition of truth, the community of needs and responsibilities. Conscience here does not mean man's openness to the basis of his being, the power of perception for what is highest and most essential. Rather, it appears as a protective shell for subjectivity into which man can escape and there hide from reality. Liberalism's idea of conscience was in fact presupposed here. Conscience does not open the way to the redemptive road to truth which either does not exist or, if it does, is too demanding. It is the faculty which dispenses from truth. It thereby becomes the justification for subjectivity, which should not be called into question. Similarly, it becomes the justification for social conformity. As mediating value between the different subjectivities, social conformity is intended to make living together possible. The obligation to seek the truth ceases, as do any doubts about the general inclination of society and what it has become accustomed to. Being convinced of oneself, as well as conforming to others, are sufficient. Man is reduced to his superficial conviction and the less depth he has, the better for him.

What I was only dimly aware of in this conversation became glaringly clear a little later in a dispute among colleagues about the justifying power of the erroneous conscience. Objecting to this thesis, someone countered that if this were so then the Nazi SS would be justified and we should seek them in heaven since they carried out all their atrocities with fanatical conviction and complete certainty of conscience. Another responded with utmost assurance that of course this was indeed the case. There is no doubting the fact that Hitler and his accomplices, who were deeply convinced of their cause, could not have acted otherwise.

Therefore, the objective terribleness of their deeds notwithstanding, they acted morally, subjectively speaking. Since they followed their albeit mistaken consciences, one would have to recognize their conduct as moral and, as a result, should not doubt their eternal salvation. Since that conversation, I knew with complete certainty that something was wrong with the theory of the justifying power of the subjective conscience; that, in other words, a concept of conscience that leads to such conclusions must be false. For subjective conviction and the lack of doubts and scruples that follow from it do not justify man. Some thirty years later, in the terse words of the psychologist Albert Gorres, I found summarized the perceptions I was trying to articulate. The elaboration of these insights forms the heart of this address. Gorres shows that the feeling of guilt, the capacity to recognize guilt, belongs essentially to the spiritual make-up of man. This feeling of guilt disturbs the false calm of conscience and could be called conscience's complaint against my self-satisfied existence. It is as necessary for man as the physical pain which signifies disturbances of normal bodily functioning. Whoever is no longer capable of perceiving guilt is spiritually ill, a "living corpse, a dramatic character's mask", as Gorres says. "Monsters, among other brutes, are the ones without guilt feelings. Perhaps Hitler did not have any, or Himmler, or Stalin. Maybe Mafia bosses do not have any guilt feelings either, or maybe their remains are just well hidden in the cellar. Even aborted guilt feelings ... All men need guilt feelings."

A look into Sacred Scripture should have precluded such diagnoses and such a theory of justification by the errant conscience. In Psalm 19:12-13, we find the interesting passage: "But who can detect their errors? Clear me from my hidden faults." That is not Old Testament objectivism, but most profound human wisdom. No longer seeing one's guilt, the falling silent of conscience in so many areas, is an even more dangerous sickness of the soul than the guilt which one still recognizes as such. He who no longer notices that killing is a sin has fallen further than the one who still recognizes the shamefulness of his actions, because the former is further removed from the truth and conversion. Not without reason does the self-righteous man in the encounter with Jesus appear as the one who is really lost. If the tax collector with all his undisputed sins stands more justified before God than the Pharisee with all his undeniably good works (Lk 18:9-14), this is not because the sins of the tax collector were not sins or the good deeds of the Pharisee not good deeds. Nor does it mean that the good that man does is not good before God, or the evil not evil or at least not particularly important. The reason for this paradoxical judgment of God is shown precisely from our question. The Pharisee no longer knows that he too has guilt. He has a completely clear conscience. But this silence of conscience makes him impenetrable to God and men, while the cry of conscience which plagues the tax collector makes him capable of truth and love. Jesus can move sinners. Not hiding behind the screen of their erroneous consciences, they have not become unreachable for the change which God expects of them, and of us. He is ineffective with the "righteous" because they are not aware of any need for forgiveness and conversion. Their consciences no longer accuse them but justify them.

We find something similar in Saint Paul who tells us that the pagans, even without the law, knew quite well what God expected of them (Rom 2:1-16). The whole theory of salvation through ignorance breaks apart with this verse. There is present in man the truth that is not to be repulsed, that one truth of the creator which in the revelation of salvation history has also been put in writing. Man can see the truth of God from the fact of his creaturehood. Not to see it is guilt. It is not seen because man does not want to see it. The "no" of the will which hinders recognition is guilt. The fact that the signal lamp does not shine is the consequence of a deliberate looking away from that which we do not wish to see.

At this point in our reflections, it is possible to draw some initial conclusions with a view to answering the question regarding the essence of conscience. We can now say: it will not do to identify man's conscience with the self-consciousness of the 'I', with its subjective certainty about itself and its moral behavior. On the one hand, this consciousness may be a mere reflection of the social surroundings and the opinions in vogue. On the other hand, it might also derive from a lack of self-criticism, a deficiency in listening to the depth of one's own soul. This diagnosis is confirmed by what has come to light since the fall of Marxist systems in Eastern Europe. The noblest and keenest minds of the liberated peoples speak of an enormous spiritual devastation which appeared in the years of the intellectual deformation. They speak of a blunting of the moral sense which is a more significant loss and danger than the economic damage which was done. The new Patriarch of Moscow stressed this poignantly in the summer of 1990. The power of perception of people who lived in a system of deception was darkened. The society lost the capacity for mercy, and human feelings were forsaken. A whole generation was lost for the good, lost for humane needs. "We must lead society back to the eternal moral values," that is to say, open ears almost gone deaf, so that once again the promptings of God might be heard in human hearts. Error, the "erring" conscience, is only at first convenient. But then the silencing of conscience leads to the dehumanization of the world and to moral danger, if one does not work against it.

To express it differently, the identification of conscience with superficial consciousness, the reduction of man to his subjectivity, does not liberate but enslaves. It makes us totally dependent on the prevailing opinions and debases these with every passing day. Whoever equates conscience with superficial conviction, identifies conscience with a pseudo-rational certainty, a certainty which in fact has been woven from self-righteousness, conformity and lethargy. Conscience is degraded to a mechanism for rationalization while it should represent the transparency of the subject for the divine, and thus constitute the very dignity and greatness of man. Conscience's reduction to subjective certitude betokens at the same time a retreat from truth. When the psalmist in anticipation of Jesus' view of sin and justice pleads for liberation from unconscious guilt, he points out that one must certainly follow an erroneous conscience. But the departure from truth which took place beforehand and now takes its revenge is the actual guilt which first lulls man into false security and then abandons him in the trackless waste.

2. Newman and Socrates: Guides to Conscience

At this juncture, I would like to make a temporary digression. Before we attempt to formulate reasonable answers to the questions regarding the essence of conscience, we must first widen the basis of our considerations somewhat, going beyond the personal which has thus far constituted our point of departure. My purpose is not to try to develop a scholarly study on the history of theories of conscience, a subject on which different contributions have appeared just recently. I would prefer rather to stay with our present approach of example and narrative. A first glance should be directed to Cardinal Newman, whose life and work could be described as a single great commentary on the question of conscience. Nor should Newman be treated in a technical way. The given framework does not permit us to evaluate the particulars of Newman's concept of conscience. I would simply like to try to indicate the place of conscience in the whole of Newman's life and thought. The insights gained from this will hopefully sharpen our view of present problems and establish the link to history, that is, both to the great witnesses of conscience and to the origin of the Christian doctrine of living according to conscience. When the subject of Newman and conscience is raised, the famous sentence from his letter to the Duke of Norfolk immediately comes to mind: "Certainly, if I am obliged to bring religion into after-dinner toasts, (which indeed does not seem quite the thing), I shall drink – to the Pope, if you please, – still to conscience first and to the Pope afterwards." In contrast to the statements of Gladstone, Newman sought to make a clear affirmation of the papacy. And in contrast to mistaken forms of ultra-Montanism, Newman embraced an interpretation of the papacy which is only correctly conceived when it is viewed together with the primacy of conscience, a papacy not put in opposition to the primacy of conscience but based on it and guaranteeing it. Modern man, who presupposes the opposition of authority to subjectivity, has difficulty understanding this. For him, conscience stands on the side of subjectivity and is the expression of the freedom of the subject. Authority, on the other hand, appears to him as the constraint on, threat to, and even the negation of freedom. So then we must go deeper to recover a vision in which this kind of opposition does not obtain.

For Newman, the middle term which establishes the connection between authority and subjectivity is truth. I do not hesitate to say that truth is the central thought of Newman's intellectual grappling. Conscience is central for him because truth stands in the middle. To put it differently, the centrality of the concept of conscience for Newman is linked to the prior centrality of the concept of truth and can only be understood from that vantage point. The dominance of the idea of conscience in Newman does not signify that he, in the nineteenth century and in contrast to "objectivistic" neo-scholasticism, espoused a philosophy or theology of subjectivity. Certainly, the subject finds in Newman an attention which it had not received in Catholic theology perhaps since St Augustine. But it is an attention in the line of Augustine and not in that of the subjectivist philosophy of the modern age. On the occasion of his elevation to cardinal, Newman declared that most of his life was a struggle against the spirit of liberalism in religion; we might add, also against Christian subjectivism, as he found it in the Evangelical movement of his time and which admittedly had provided him with the first step on his lifelong road to conversion. Conscience for Newman does not mean that the subject is the standard *vis-à-vis* the claims of authority in a truthless world, a world which lives from the compromise between the claims of the subject and the claims of the social order. Even more, conscience signifies the perceptible and demanding presence of the voice of truth in the subject himself. It is the overcoming of mere subjectivity in the encounter of the interiority of man with the truth from God. The verse Newman composed in 1833 in Sicily is characteristic: "I loved to choose and see my path but now, lead thou me on!" Newman's conversion to Catholicism was not for him a matter of personal taste or of subjective, spiritual need. He expressed himself on this even in 1844, on the threshold, so to speak, of his conversion: "No one can have a more unfavorable view than I of the present state of Roman Catholics." Newman was much more taken by the necessity to obey recognized truth than his own preferences – even against his own sensitivity and bonds of friendship and ties due to similar backgrounds. It seems to me characteristic of Newman that he emphasized the priority of truth over goodness in the order of virtues. Or, to put it in a way which is more understandable for us, he emphasized truth's priority over consensus, over the accommodation of groups. I would say that when we are speaking of a man of conscience, we mean one who looks at things this way. A man of conscience is one who never acquires tolerance, well-being, success, public standing, and approval on the part of prevailing opinion, at the expense of truth. In this respect, Newman is related to Britain's other great witness of conscience, Thomas More, for whom conscience was not at all an expression of subjective stubbornness or obstinate heroism. He numbered himself, in fact, among those fainthearted martyrs who only after faltering and much questioning succeed in mustering up obedience to conscience, mustering up obedience to the truth which must stand higher than any human tribunal or any type of personal taste. Thus two standards become apparent for ascertaining the presence of a real voice of conscience. First, conscience is not identical to personal wishes and taste. Secondly, conscience cannot be reduced to social advantage, to group consensus or to the demands of political and social power.

Let us take a side-look now at the situation of our day. The individual may not achieve his advancement or well-being at the cost of betraying what he recognizes to be true, nor may humanity. Here we come in contact with the really critical issue of the modern age. The concept of truth has been virtually given up and replaced by the concept of progress. Progress itself *is* truth. But through this seeming exaltation, progress loses its direction and becomes nullified. For if no direction exists, everything can just as well be to regress as to progress. Einstein's theory of relativity properly concerns the physical cosmos. But it seems to me to describe exactly the situation of the intellectual/spiritual world of our time. The theory of relativity states there are no fixed systems of reference in the universe. When we declare a system to be a reference point from which we try to measure a whole, it is we who do the determining. Only in such a way can we attain any results at all. But the determination could always have been done differently. What we said about the physical cosmos is reflected in the second "Copernican revolution" regarding our basic relationship to reality. The truth as such, the absolute, the very reference point of thinking, is no longer visible. For this reason, precisely in the spiritual sense, there is no longer "up or down." There are no directions in a world without fixed measuring points. What we view to be direction is not based on a standard which is true in itself but on our decision and finally on considerations of expediency. In such a relativistic context, any so-called teleological or consequentialist ethics ultimately become nihilistic, even if it fails to see this. And what is called conscience in such a worldview is, on deeper reflection, but a euphemistic way of saying that there is no such thing as an actual conscience, conscience understood as a "co-knowing" with the truth. Each person determines his own standards. And, needless to say, in general relativity, no one can be of much help to the other, much less prescribe behavior to him.

At this point, the whole radicality of today's dispute over ethics and conscience, its centre, becomes plain. It seems to me that the parallel in the history of thought is the quarrel between Socrates-Plato and the sophists in which the fateful decision between two fundamental positions has been rehearsed. There is, on the one hand, the position of confidence in man's capacity for truth. On the other, there is a worldview in which man alone sets standards for himself. The fact that Socrates, the pagan, could become in a certain respect the prophet of Jesus Christ has its roots in this fundamental question. In taking up of this question based on the way of philosophizing, Socrates inspired in himself a kind of salvation-historical privilege and made it an appropriate vessel for the Christian Logos. For with the Christian Logos we are dealing with liberation through truth and to truth. If you isolate Socrates' dispute from the accidents of the time and take into account his use of other arguments and terminology, you begin to see how closely this is the same dilemma we face today. Giving up the idea of man's capacity for truth leads first to pure formalism in the use of words and concepts. Again, the loss of content, then and now, leads to a pure formalism of judgment. Today, for example, many people no longer bother to ask what a person thinks. The verdict on someone's thinking is readily at hand as long as you can give it its corresponding formal category: conservative, reactionary, fundamentalist, progressive, revolutionary. Assignment to a formal scheme suffices to render coming to terms with the content unnecessary. The same thing can be seen, in more concentrated form, in art. What a work of art says is indifferent. It can glorify God or the devil. The sole standard is that of formal, technical mastery.

We now have arrived at the heart of the matter. Where contents no longer count, where pure praxeology takes over, technique becomes the main criterion. This means, though, that power becomes the preeminent category, whether revolutionary or reactionary. This is precisely the distorted form of being like God of which the account of the fall speaks. The way of mere technical skill, the way of sheer power, is imitation of an idol and not expression of one's being made in the image and likeness of God. What characterizes man as man is not that he asks about the "can" but about the "should" and that he opens himself to the voice and demands of truth. It seems to me that this was the final meaning of the Socratic search and it is the profoundest element in the witness of all martyrs. They attest to the fact that man's capacity for truth is a limit on all power and a guarantee of man's likeness to God. It is precisely in this way that the martyrs are the great witnesses of conscience, of that capability given to man to perceive the "should" beyond the "can" and thereby render possible real progress, real ascent.

3. Systematic Consequences: The two levels of Conscience

(a) Anamnesis

After all these ramblings through intellectual history, it is finally time to arrive at some conclusions: that is, to formulate a concept of conscience. The medieval tradition was right, I believe, in according two levels to the concept of conscience. These levels, though they can be well distinguished, must be continually referred to each other. It seems to me that many unacceptable theses regarding conscience are the result of neglecting either the difference or the connection between the two. Mainstream scholasticism expressed these two levels in the concepts synderesis and conscientia. The word synderesis (synteresis) came into the medieval tradition of conscience from the stoic doctrine of the microcosm. It remained unclear in its exact meaning and for this reason became a hindrance to a careful development of this essential aspect of the whole question of conscience. I would like, therefore, without entering into philosophical disputes, to replace this problematic word with the much more clearly defined Platonic concept of anamnesis. It is not only linguistically clearer and philosophically deeper and purer, but anamnesis above all also harmonizes with key motifs of biblical thought and the anthropology derived therefrom. The word anamnesis should be taken to mean exactly what Paul expressed in the second chapter of his Letter to the Romans: "When Gentiles who have not the law do by nature what the law requires, they are a law to themselves, even though they do not have the law. They show that what the law requires is written on their hearts while their conscience also bears witness ..." (2:14 f.). The same thought is strikingly amplified in the great monastic rule of Saint Basil. Here we read: "The love of God is not founded on a discipline imposed on us from outside, but is constitutively established in us as the capacity and necessity of our rational nature." Basil speaks in terms of "the spark of divine love which has been hidden in us", an expression which was to become important in medieval mysticism. In the spirit of Johannine theology, Basil knows that love consists in keeping the commandments. For this reason, the spark of love which has been put into us by the Creator means this: "We have received interiorly beforehand the capacity and disposition for observing all divine commandments ...These are not something imposed from without." Referring everything back to its simple core, Augustine adds: "We could never judge that one thing is better than another if a basic understanding of the good had not already been instilled in us."

This means that the first so-called ontological level of the phenomenon of conscience consists in the fact that something like an original memory of the good and true (they are identical) has been implanted in us, that there is an inner ontological tendency within man, who is created in the likeness of God, toward the divine. From its origin, man's being resonates with some things and clashes with others. This anamnesis of the origin, which results from the godlike constitution of our being, is not a conceptually articulated knowing, a store of retrievable contents. It is an inner sense, a capacity to recall, so that the one whom it addresses, if he is not turned in on himself, hears its echo from within. He sees: "That's it! That is what my nature points to and seeks."

The possibility of and the right to "mission" rest on this anamnesis of the creator that is identical to the ground of our existence. The Gospel may - indeed must – be proclaimed to the pagans because they themselves are yearning for it in the hidden recesses of their souls (cf. Is 42:4). Mission is vindicated then when those addressed recognize in the encounter with the word of the Gospel that this indeed is what they have been waiting for. In this sense, Paul can say: the Gentiles are a law to themselves – not in the sense of modern liberal notions of autonomy which preclude transcendence of the subject, but in the much deeper sense that nothing belongs less to me than I myself. My own I is the site of the profoundest surpassing of self and contact with Him from whom I came and toward whom I am going. In these sentences, Paul expresses the experience which he had as missionary to the Gentiles and which Israel may have experienced before him in dealings with the "god-fearing". Israel could have experienced among the Gentiles what the ambassadors of Jesus Christ found reconfirmed. Their proclamation answered an expectation. Their proclamation encountered an antecedent basic knowledge of the essential constants of the will of God which came to be written down in the commandments, which can be found in all cultures. They can be all the more clearly elucidated the less an overbearing cultural bias distorts this primordial knowledge. The more man lives in the "fear of the Lord" – consider the story of Cornelius (especially Acts 10:34-35) – the more concretely and clearly effective this anamnesis becomes.

Again, let us take a formulation of St Basil. The love of God, which is concrete in the commandments, is not imposed on us from without, the Church Father emphasizes, but has been implanted in us beforehand. As Augustine says, the sense for the good has been stamped upon us. We can now appreciate Newman's toast first to conscience and then to the Pope. The Pope cannot impose commandments on faithful Catholics because he wants to or finds it expedient. Such a modern, voluntaristic concept of authority can only distort the true theological meaning of the papacy. The true nature of the Petrine office has become so incomprehensible in the modern age no doubt because we only think of authority in terms which do not allow for bridges between subject and object. Accordingly, everything which does not come from the subject is thought to be externally imposed. But the situation is really quite different according to the anthropology of conscience which through these reflections we have hopefully appreciated. The anamnesis instilled in our being needs, one might say, assistance from without so that it can become aware of itself. But this "from without" is not something set in opposition to anamnesis but ordered to it. It has a maieutic function, imposes nothing foreign, but brings to fruition what is proper to anamnesis, namely its interior openness to the truth.

When we are dealing with the question of faith and church whose radius extends from the redeeming Logos over the gift of creation, we must, however, take into account yet another dimension which is especially developed in the Johannine writings. John is familiar with the anamnesis of the new "we" which is granted to us in the incorporation into Christ (one Body, i.e., one "I" with Him). In remembering they knew him, so the Gospel has it in a number of places. The original encounter with Jesus gave the disciples what all generations thereafter receive in their foundational encounter with the Lord in Baptism and the Eucharist, namely, the new anamnesis of faith which unfolds, similarly to the anamnesis of creation, in constant dialogue between within and without.

In contrast to the presumption of Gnostic teachers who wanted to convince the faithful that their naive faith must be understood and applied very differently, John could say: you do not need such instruction, for as anointed ones (i.e., baptized) you know everything (cf. 1 Jn 2:20). This does not mean a factual omniscience on the part of the faithful. It does signify, however, the sureness of the Christian memory. This Christian memory, to be sure, is always learning, but proceeding from its sacramental identity it also distinguishes from within between what is a genuine unfolding of its recollection and what is its destruction or falsification. In the crisis of the Church today, the power of this recollection and the truth of the apostolic word is experienced in an entirely new way, where much more than hierarchical direction, it is the power of memory of the simple faith which leads to the discernment of spirits. One can only comprehend the primacy of the Pope and its correlation to Christian conscience in this connection. The true sense of this teaching authority of the Pope consists in his being the advocate of the Christian memory. The Pope does not impose from without. Rather, he elucidates the Christian memory and defends it. For this reason the toast to conscience indeed must precede the toast to the Pope because without conscience there would not be a papacy. All power that the papacy has is power of conscience. It is service to the double memory upon which the faith is based and which again and again must be purified, expanded and defended against the destruction of memory which is threatened by a subjectivity forgetful of its own foundation as well as by the pressures of social and cultural conformity.

(b) Conscientia

Having considered this first, essentially ontological, level of the concept of conscience, we must now turn to its second level: that of judgment and decision which the medieval tradition designates with the single word *conscientia,* conscience. Presumably this terminological tradition has not insignificantly contributed to the diminution of the concept of conscience. Thomas, for example, only designates this second level as *conscientia.* For him it stands to reason that conscience is not a *habitus,* that is a lasting *ontic* quality of man, but *actus,* an event in execution. Thomas of course assumes as given, the ontological foundation of anamnesis (synderesis). He describes anamnesis as an inner repugnance to evil and an attraction to the good. The act of conscience applies this basic knowledge to the particular situation. According to Thomas it is divided into three elements: recognizing *(recognoscere),* bearing witness *(testificari),* and finally judging *(judicare).* One might speak of an interaction between a function of control and a function of decision. Thomas sees this sequence according to the Aristotelian model of deductive reasoning. But he is careful to emphasize what is peculiar to this knowledge of moral actions whose conclusions do not come from mere knowing or thinking. Whether something is recognized or not, depends also on the will which can block the way to recognition or lead to it. It is dependent on an already formed moral character which can either continue to deform or be further purified. On this level, the level of judgment (conscientia in the narrower sense), it can be said that even the erroneous conscience binds. This statement is completely intelligible from the rational tradition of scholasticism. No-one may act against his convictions, as St Paul had already said (Rom 14:23). But the fact that the conviction a person has come to certainly binds in the moment of acting, does not signify a canonization of subjectivity. It is never wrong to follow the convictions one has arrived at – in fact, one must do so. But it can very well be wrong to have come to such askew convictions in the first place, by having stifled the protest of the anamnesis of being. The guilt lies then in a different place, much deeper – not in the present act, not in the present judgment of conscience, but in the neglect of my being which made me deaf to the internal promptings of truth. For this reason, criminals of conviction like Hitler and Stalin are guilty. These crass examples should not serve to put us at ease but should rouse us to take seriously the earnestness of the plea: "Free me from my unknown guilt" (Ps 19:13).

Epilogue: Conscience and Grace

At the end, there remains the question with which we began. Is not the truth, at least as the faith of the Church shows it to us, too lofty and difficult for man? Taking into consideration everything we have said, we can respond as follows. Certainly the high road to truth and goodness is not a comfortable one. It challenges man. Nevertheless, retreat into self, however comfortable, does not redeem. The self withers away and becomes lost. But in ascending the heights of the good, man discovers more and more the beauty which lies in the arduousness of truth which constitutes redemption for him. We would dissolve Christianity into moralism if no message which surpasses our own actions became discernible. Without many words, an image from the Greek world can show this to us. In it we can observe simultaneously both how the anamnesis of the creator extends from within us outward towards the redeemer, and how everyone may see him as redeemer because he answers our own innermost expectations. I am speaking of the story of the expiation of the sin of matricide of Orestes. He had committed the murder as an act of conscience. This is designated by the mythological language of obedience to the command of the god Apollo. But he now finds himself hounded by the Furies or Erinyes who are to be seen as mythological personifications of conscience that, from a deeper wellspring of recollection, reproach Orestes, declaring that his decision of conscience, his obedience to the "saying of the gods", was in reality guilt.

The whole tragedy of man comes to light in this dispute of the "gods," that is to say, in this conflict of conscience. In the holy court, the white stone of Athena leads to Orestes' acquittal, his sanctification, in the power of which the Erinyes are transformed into spirits of reconciliation. Atonement has transformed the world. The myth, while representing the transition from a system of blood vengeance to the right order of community, signifies much more than just that. Hans Urs von Balthasar expressed this "more" as follows: "... Calming grace always assists in the establishing of justice, not the old graceless justice of the Erinyes period, but that which is full of grace..." This myth speaks to us of the human longing that conscience's objectively just indictment, and the attendant destructive, interior distress it causes in man, should not be the last word. It thus speaks of an authority of grace, a power of expiation which allows the guilt to vanish and makes truth at last truly redemptive. It is the longing for a truth which doesn't just make demands of us but also transforms us through expiation and pardon. Through these, as Aeschylus puts it, "guilt is washed away" and our being is transformed from within, beyond our own capability. This is the real innovation of Christianity.

The Logos, the truth in person, is also the atonement, the transforming forgiveness above and beyond our capability and incapability. Therein lies the real novelty upon which the larger Christian memory is founded and which indeed, at the same time, constitutes the deeper answer to what the anamnesis of the creator expects of us. Where this centre of the Christian anamnesis is not sufficiently expressed and appreciated, truth becomes a yoke which is too heavy for our shoulders and from which we must seek to free ourselves. But the freedom gained thereby is empty. It leads into the desolate land of nothingness and disintegrates of itself. Yet the yoke of truth in fact became "easy" (Mt 11:30) when the truth came, loved us, and consumed our guilt in the fire of his love. Only when we know and experience this from within, will we be free to hear the message of conscience with joy and without fear.

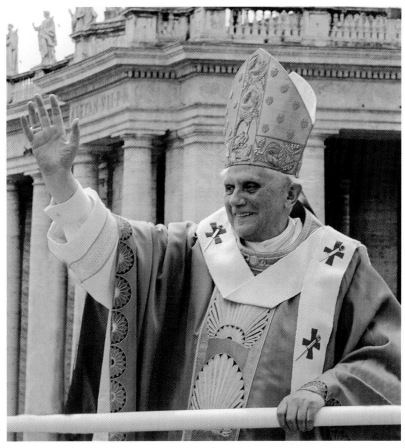

Benedict XVI after his Inaugural Mass in St Peter's Square, Sunday 24 April 2005.

Fotografia Felici

Cardinal Newman, photograph c. 1885.

Courtesy of the Fathers of the Birmingham Oratory

Part four

Newman as seen by others

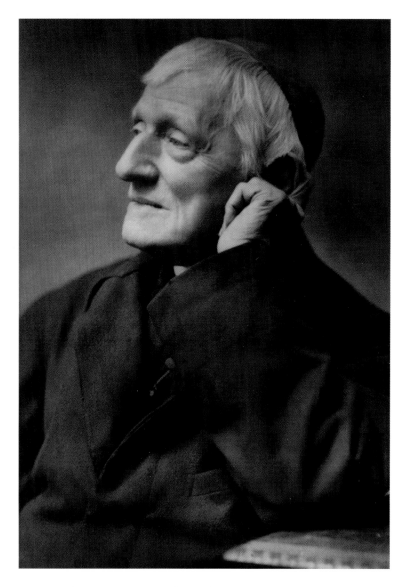

John Henry Newman by Herbert Rose Barraud c. 1882.

Courtesy of the Fathers of the Birmingham Oratory

The importance of Newman today

Cardinal Cormac Murphy O'Connor

The great saint-intellectuals of history transcend their epochs. Almost anyone can come casually to St Augustine's *Confessions*, even from the distance of a thousand years, and know the thrill of a journey into the arms of God. The same could be said of Newman's *Apologia pro vita sua*.

But what, specifically, does Newman have to say to us today – especially about the ecclesiological debates of our time?

Newman's was the holiest intellect in nineteenth-century England. He enquired, with searing honesty, into the great questions of the Church and the Christian faith, first as the driving force of the Tractarian movement, which aimed to restore to Anglicanism its share in the Catholic tradition, and later when he was drawn by his own arguments, inexorably and at great personal cost, into the Catholic Church itself. But his story goes much deeper. His *Apologia* is in essence a pilgrim's tale – the story of a heart, and an intellect, with a firm purpose to discover God's specific need of him, through both his triumphs and his failures, his weaknesses as well as his strengths.

As Newman said in a sermon in 1849: "We are not sent into this world for nothing; we are not born at random; we are not here that we may go to bed at night, and get up in the morning, toil for our bread, eat and drink, laugh and joke, sin when we have a mind, and reform when we are tired of sinning, rear a family and die. God sees every one of us; He creates every soul, . . . for a purpose. He needs, He deigns to need, every one of us. He has an end for each of us; we are all equal in His sight, and we are placed in our different ranks and stations, not to get what we can out of them for ourselves, but to labour in them for Him. As Christ has His work, we too have ours; as He rejoiced to do His work, we must rejoice in ours also."[1]

Newman's work was intellectual enquiry underpinned by a soul's restless search for his Maker. In the process he leaped across boundaries, earning suspicion and hostility. His reception into the Catholic Church caused friends to abandon him; his plans for the Oratory in Birmingham were scarred by an unhappy dispute; he was tried and found guilty of libel – a verdict which prompted *The Times*, no friend then of Rome, to observe that Roman Catholics could no longer have faith in British justice. He was invited to found a university in Dublin, but was denied the support he needed to make it a success. He came under suspicion in Rome for his article on the laity, but his defence was never passed on to church authorities, leaving him under a cloud there. His plans for an Oratory in Oxford were encouraged and then frustrated. His position on papal infallibility brought him into conflict with the ultramontane Cardinal Manning. And so on.

But towards the end of his life Newman was vindicated. Friendships with the Tractarians

---

[1] Sermon: 'God's Will the End of Life', from *Discourses Addressed to Mixed Congregations* (1849), in Daniel M O'Connell, *Favorite Newman Sermons*, 2nd ed. (New York, The America Press, 1940) pp. 177-178.

were healed. He was made a fellow of Trinity College after more than thirty years of rejection. And in 1879 he was made a cardinal by Pope Leo XIII. His love of truth and of Christ triumphed over misunderstanding and suspicion, and his saintly qualities achieved ever greater recognition after his death.

Newman's theology came into its own, however, with the Second Vatican Council. The Council restored the value of the local Church embedded in local culture, but no less for that part of the universal Body: it is Newman who shows us still how best to be both English and Catholic. The Council also restored the place of the laity, without whom, as Newman once drily observed, the Church would look a little odd. Newman's famous article, "On Consulting the Christian faithful in matters of doctrine", remains a personal favourite of mine, and a guiding light for me as a bishop. Newman bequeathed some of his most enduring passages on lay people, especially in his remarks on the hiddenness of God's saints and their influence. "Say they are few, such high Christians; and what follows? They are enough to carry on God's noiseless work."[2]

All these contributions would be enough to command attention from contemporary Catholics. To say that Newman bears re-reading is almost to utter a cliché. His mysticism – those lyrical passages in which he uncovers God's providence, the unseen, but closely felt, presence of the divine in the world – would be enough to rank him among the greatest in the Christian tradition. Never has an Englishman so completely set forth so complete an account of Christian faith as did Newman in his lifetime.

But it is in his role as an ecumenist that I believe his greatest significance for today's Church lies. His patristic work, devoted mainly to St Athanasius and the Alexandrian School, has marked the field forever;[3] but it was also decisive in his own journey into the Catholic Church. No one in Britain has ever inquired so deeply, and with greater integrity, into ecclesiology – the mechanism by which Jesus Christ, in founding a Church, guaranteed the preservation and ongoing revelation of faith – as did Newman. Anglicans, and those, such as myself, whose role has been to maintain with them a cooperative but honest dialogue, have been unable to avoid those dilemmas which have persisted, with often dramatic consequences, to this day.

Newman speaks to these directly, for in his enquiry into the very heart of the notion of Church he wrestled with the questions which today underpin debates in the Churches. The debate over the ordination of women in the Church of England – in the early 1990s as priests; more recently as bishops – and the recent question of how the Anglican Communion is to establish its borders when one member Church defies the wishes of the Primates, are of a piece with the debates in Newman's day. It is hard, indeed, to read the *Windsor Report*, as the conclusions of the commission chaired by Lord Eames into this last issue are known, without thinking of Newman. His shadow hangs over the Synods and the Commissions.

But his ecclesiological enquiries are as valid for Catholics as for Anglicans. He became deeply involved in the question of papal infallibility, which was for Englishmen of the

---

[2] See Mgr Roderick Strange's 'Newman's Influence: A Personal Reflection', Ho Teologos 8 (1990) pp. 65 - 76.

[3] For a contemporary valuation of Newman's contribution to patristics, see Archbishop Rowan Williams's book *Arius: Heresy and Tradition* 2nd ed. (London, 2001).

time the great challenge of the Catholic Church. His was a "fine historical sensitivity", as Mgr Strange describes it, "which refused to be trapped in the particular moment, but maintained the longer perspective"[4]. He saw popes as continually completing the acts of their predecessors, refining and defining the Councils, whose utterances were *de fide* in as much as they were rooted in the eternal dogmas of the Church. "Dogma" was not a word Newman was afraid of – in contrast to many of his liberal contemporaries, who saw it as arbitrary and authoritarian. Newman arrived at the opposite view: Catholic dogma was for him the guarantee of freedom, the "fundamental principle" of religion, as he described it in the *Apologia*. For Newman orthodoxy was the lubricant of theological enquiry. Critical theology was the antidote both to infallibilist extremism, and to the liberal error, "the exercise of thought upon matters, in which, from the constitution of the human mind, thought cannot be brought to any successful issue, and is therefore out of place" (*Apologia* 288).

His marriage of intellect and dogma is a challenge to those of our contemporaries for whom the act of faith appears as a surrender of freedom and autonomy. His famous teaching that ten thousand difficulties do not add up to a single doubt is a wonderful reassertion of St Augustine's formula that in the inessential there needs to be liberty, while in the essential, unity. Intellectual difficulties in the journey of faith are not to be feared or rejected as symptoms of unbelief; they are the natural result of the human mind being drawn closer into the unfathomable mystery of God.

Indeed, Newman is the friend of the contemporary enquirer into faith. But he warns us against the Enlightenment myth of the sole searcher, in which proximity to truth occurs in isolation. Few people have made more personal sacrifices, for the sake of truth, than Newman; yet he maintained, following the pattern of Jesus Christ, that "the best preparation for loving the world at large, and loving it duly and wisely, is to cultivate an intimate friendship and affection towards those who are immediately about us". The idea, of course, is sacramental; and no one would have been more delighted with the postconciliar theology of *communio* than Newman.

That is why he is a sure guide through the thickets of modern ecclesiological debates. For so often those debates turn on antithetical ideas: prophecy versus unity; Scripture versus tradition; freedom versus authority. It is common, in both the Anglican and the Catholic Churches, to assume that prophecy is antagonistic to the offices of governance in the Church. Newman's own life – he was for a time under a cloud in Rome yet vindicated by Leo XIII in 1879 – would appear to prove as much. Yet in the preface he wrote as a Catholic to a reprint of his Anglican work, *Via Media*, prophecy is never a radical counterbalance to institutional religion. As John McDade puts it, prophecy for Newman "is how the Church comes to be bound to the gospel of Christ because it enables the apostolic proclamation to be received deeply by human beings, thereby creating a believing body enlivened by its faith in Christ." Prophets in Newman's writings are "interpreters of revelation", who "unfold" and "define" its mysteries, "illuminating", "harmonising", and "applying" them. The prophetic tradition of the Church is not outside apostolic tradition (Scripture, credal formulae, conciliar decrees, sacraments), but is the

---

[4] See R Strange, 'Newman on Infallibility', Ampleforth Journal LXXX (Spring, 1975), pp. 61-70.

Gospel lived, as it were, "all over the place":

"Their teaching is a vast system, not to be comprised in a few sentences, not to be embodied in one code or treatise, but consisting of a certain body of Truth, pervading the Church like an atmosphere, irregular in its shape from its very profusion and exuberance; at times separable only in idea from Episcopal Tradition, yet at times melting away into legend and fable; partly written, partly unwritten, partly preserved in intellectual expressions, partly latent in the spirit and temper of Christians; poured to and fro in closets and upon the housetops, in liturgies, in controversial works, in obscure fragments, in sermons, in popular prejudices, in local customs."[5]

Running beneath these words is the familiar Gospel idea that God has revealed to "mere children" what is hidden from the wise and the learned (Mt 12:25) or Paul's reminder to the Corinthians that "God chose what is low and despised in this world" to witness to his power (1 Cor 1:26). Newman is thus giving valuable testimony to the dynamism of Christianity in producing a multi-layered culture, a "common fund" of story, memory and values available to all – what in the Catholic Church has traditionally been spoken of as *sentire cum ecclesia*.

Newman's grasp of the value of a common culture needs to be understood and re-asserted as never before in our own time and place. The culture of the world around us is one which deliberately weakens the bond between individuals and communities of meaning and value, in order to promote the idea of the autonomous self. That idea, of course, is a chimera, one which in the name of autonomy persuades isolated individuals to conform to consumerist ideals. But the idea is effective enough to imbue society with the presumption that the individual standing boldly apart from the institution is an unqualified good, and conformity bad – a hierarchy of values that has necessarily influenced the way in which modern Catholics and Anglicans regard themselves in relation to the Body of which they form a part.

The consequences of this have been especially felt in recent times in the Anglican Communion, and it is hard not to believe that a re-reading of Newman would help in its deliberations over the *Windsor Report*.

But Newman's faith in the *sensus communis* is also relevant for the question of collegiality in the Catholic Church. Never Peter without the eleven, nor the eleven without Peter – this is the principle which underlines the governance of the Church by the bishops "with and under the Pope". The bishops are the Vicars of Christ in their dioceses, but also represent the local to the universal Church, giving voice to "a certain body of Truth, pervading the Church like an atmosphere" which pertains in each diocese.

There are, in sum, few better guides to true ecclesiology than Newman, and therefore no better companion for contemporary ecumenists. His engagement with the great questions of his time was total. But the deeper significance of his explorations may yet become visible more than ever in our own time.

---

[5] From the 1877 preface which Newman wrote, as a Catholic, to the reprint of *Via Media*.

A nineteenth century portrait of Newman, which hangs in the Cardinals' Corridor in the Venerable English College, Rome, where Cardinal Murphy-O'Connor was a student and later Rector.

Courtesy of the Rector of the Venerable English College

William Bernard Ullathorne OSB, an English Benedictine monk, was appointed as the first Bishop of Birmingham, following the restoration of the English Hierarchy by Pope Pius IX on 29 September 1850. He had a long friendship with Newman. He died at Oscott College on 21 March 1889.

Courtesy of the Fathers of the Birmingham Oratory

Apologia pro vita sua

Post scriptum

4 June 1864

While I was engaged with these concluding pages, I received another of those special encouragements, which from several quarters have been bestowed upon me, since my controversy began. It was the extraordinary honour done me of an address from the clergy of this large diocese, who had been assembled for the Synod.

It was followed two days afterwards by a most gracious testimonial from my bishop, Dr Ullathorne, in the shape of a letter which he wrote to me, and also inserted in the Birmingham papers. With his leave I transfer it to my own volume, as a very precious document, completing and recompensing, in a way most grateful to my feelings, the anxious work which has occupied me so fully for nearly ten weeks.

Bishop's House, 2 June 1864

My dear Dr Newman,

It was with warm gratification that, after the close of the Synod yesterday, I listened to the Address presented to you by the clergy of the diocese, and to your impressive reply. But I should have been little satisfied with the part of the silent listener, except on the understanding with myself that I also might afterwards express to you my own sentiments in my own way.

We have now been personally acquainted, and much more than acquainted, for nineteen years, during more than sixteen of which we have stood in special relation of duty towards each other. This has been one of the singular blessings which God has given me amongst the cares of the Episcopal office. What my feelings of respect, of confidence, and of affection have been towards you, you know well; nor should I think of expressing them in words. But there is one thing that has struck me in this day of explanations, which you could not, and would not, be disposed to do, and which no one could do so properly or so authentically as I could, and which it seems to me is not altogether uncalled for, if every kind of erroneous impression that some persons have entertained with no better evidence than conjecture is to be removed.

It is difficult to comprehend how, in the face of facts, the notion should ever have arisen that during your Catholic life, you have been more occupied with your own thoughts than with the service of religion and the work of the Church. If we take no other work into consideration beyond the written productions which your Catholic pen has given to the world, they are enough for the life's labour of another. There are the Lectures on Anglican Difficulties, the Lectures on Catholicism in England, the great work on the Scope and End of University Education, that on the Office and Work of Universities, the Lectures and Essays on University Subjects, and the two Volumes of

Sermons; not to speak of your contributions to the *Atlantis*, which you founded, and to other periodicals; then there are those beautiful offerings to Catholic literature, the *Lectures on the Turks, Loss and Gain,* and *Callista*, and though last, not least, the *Apologia*, which is destined to put many idle rumours to rest, and many unprofitable surmises; and yet all these productions represent but a portion of your labour, and that in the second half of your period of public life.

These works have been written in the midst of labour and cares of another kind, and of which the world knows very little. I will specify four of these undertakings, each of a distinct character, and any one of which would have made a reputation for untiring energy in the practical order.

The first of these undertakings was the establishment of the congregation of the Oratory of St. Philip Neri – that great ornament and accession to the force of English Catholicity. Both the London and the Birmingham Oratory must look to you as their founder and as the originator of their characteristic excellences; whilst that of Birmingham has never known any other presidency.

No sooner was this work fairly on foot than you were called by the highest authority to commence another, and one of yet greater magnitude and difficulty, the founding of a University in Ireland. After the Universities had been lost to the Catholics of these kingdoms for three centuries, every thing had to be begun from the beginning: the idea of such an institution to be inculcated, the plan to be formed that would work, the resources to be gathered, and the staff of superiors and professors to be brought together. Your name was then the chief point of attraction which brought these elements together. You alone know what difficulties you had to conciliate and what to surmount, before the work reached that state of consistency and promise, which enabled you to return to those responsibilities in England which you had never laid aside or suspended.

The original plan of an Oratory did not contemplate any parochial work, but you could not contemplate so many souls in want of pastors without being prompt and ready at the beck of authority to strain all your efforts in coming to their help. And this brings me to the third and the most continuous of those labours to which I have alluded. The mission in Alcester Street, its church and schools, were the first work of the Birmingham Oratory. After several years of close and hard work, and a considerable call upon the private resources of the Fathers who had established this congregation, it was delivered over to other hands, and the Fathers removed to the district of Edgbaston, where up to that time nothing Catholic had appeared. Then arose under your direction the large convent of the Oratory, the church expanded by degrees into its present capaciousness, a numerous congregation has gathered and grown in it; poor schools and other pious institutions have grown up in connexion with it, and, moreover, equally at your expense and that of your brethren, and, as I have reason to know, at much inconvenience, the Oratory has relieved the other clergy of Birmingham all this while by constantly doing the duty in the poor-house and gaol of Birmingham.

More recently still, the mission and the poor school at Smethwick owe their existence to the Oratory. And all this while the founder and father of these religious works has added to his other solicitudes the toil of frequent preaching, of attendance in the confessional, and other parochial duties.

I have read on this day of its publication the seventh part of the *Apologia,* and the touching allusion in it to the devotedness of the Catholic clergy to the poor in seasons of pestilence reminds me that when the cholera raged so dreadfully at Bilston, and the two priests of the town were no longer equal to the number of cases to which they were hurried day and night, I asked you to lend me two fathers to supply the place of other priests whom I wished to send as a further aid. But you and Father St John preferred to take the place of danger which I had destined for others, and remained at Bilston till the worst was over.

The fourth work which I would notice is one more widely known. I refer to the school for the education of the higher classes, which at the solicitation of many friends yon have founded and attached to the Oratory. Surely after reading this bare enumeration of work done, no man will venture to say that Dr. Newman is leading a comparatively inactive life in the service of the Church.

To spare, my dear Dr Newman, any further pressure on those feelings with which I have already taken so large a liberty, I will only add one word more for my own satisfaction. During our long intercourse there is only one subject on which, after the first experience, I have measured my words with some caution, and that has been where questions bearing on ecclesiastical duty have arisen. I found some little caution necessary, because you were always so prompt and ready to go even beyond the slightest intimation of my wish or desires.

That God may bless you with health, life, and all the spiritual good which you desire, you and your brethren of the Oratory, is the earnest prayer now and often of, my dear Dr Newman, your affectionate friend and faithful servant in Christ,

+ W B Ullathorne.

This *Post Scriptum* is not included in all editions of *Apologia pro vita sua.*

Archbishop Ullathorne was Bishop in the Midlands during forty years of Newman's life there, first as Vicar Apostolic of the Central District, then as first Bishop of Birmingham, 1848–1888. He was made a titular Archbishop when he retired, but died shortly afterwards on 21 March 1889. He wrote to Newman only a month before his own death – on 21 February 1889 – sending the Cardinal greetings on his birthday. Newman had preached at his installation.

Archbishop Vincent Nichols of Birmingham greeting Pope Benedict XVI in the Paul VI Hall, at the end of an audience which the newly elected Pope gave to members of the media on Saturday 23 April 2005.

Fotografia Felici

Pope Benedict XVI was greeted by warm applause from more than two-thousand members of the world's media, including Rome-based correspondents accredited to the Holy See Press Office. He spoke in Italian, English, French and German during the sixteen-minute audience.

Speaking in English, Pope Benedict said: "Thanks to all of you, these historically important ecclesial events have had world-wide coverage. I know how hard you have worked, far away from your homes and families, for long hours and in sometimes difficult conditions. I am aware of the skill and dedication with which you have accomplished your demanding task. In my own name, and especially on behalf of Catholics living far from Rome, who were unable to participate in these stirring moments for our faith as they were taking place, I thank you for all you have done. The possibilities opened up for us by modern means of social communication are indeed marvellous and extaordinary!"

Newman's pastoral work in Birmingham

Vincent Nichols, Archbishop of Birmingham

There are many aspects to the life of Cardinal John Henry Newman and many facets to his personality. Some are well known and widely appreciated. This is particularly true of his immense output of written work and, of course, of his great journey of conscience. He is well known, too, as an innovator and founder, as a man of considerable vision and determination.

Yet there is another aspect to his life which also needs to be widely appreciated if the picture is to be complete. This is certainly the case in any reflection on the holiness of the Venerable John Henry Newman.

It is his work as priest in the parish which needs bringing into the picture. For over forty years he worked steadfastly and generously in Birmingham as a priest of the Oratory, offering to the people all the customary ministry of a priest. He brought to that ministry all his exceptional gifts. And his ministry was widely appreciated.

It is this aspect of the life and holiness of John Henry Newman which can add significantly to his appeal to people today. Here was a man of international academic repute, a man used to moving in the highest circles, yet who devoted himself, tirelessly, to the care of some of the poorest and most burdened people of the city he had made his own.

This, I believe, is a great encouragement. It is so for parishioners today, for it reminds us that the work of God in our world finds its first expressions in the ordinariness of daily lives. God is to be found, together with the grace and comfort which faith in God brings, precisely amidst the burdens and joys of daily routines. This, of course, is a central thrust of the Gospel, bringing to clarity and fulfilment all that was promised to the People of Israel.

In Psalm 112 (113) for example, the great call to praise is motivated, in part at least, by the incontrovertible love of the Lord for the least:

> Who is like the Lord our God
> > who is seated on high
> > who looks far down
> > > on the heavens and the earth?

> He raises the poorest from the dust
> > and lifts the needy from the ash heap
> > to make them sit with princes
> > > with the princes of his people. (vv. 5–8)

Here not only is the majesty and glory of God strongly affirmed, but also God's compassion, God's tender loving care. In God's sight no one is insignificant; no one is too lowly or poor to count. In today's world testimony to this truth is much needed.

This Psalm finds strong echoes in Mary's own hymn of praise. She is, *par excellence*, the 'lowly one'. In raising her up God not only fulfils that earlier promise but also establishes the means by which God himself will embrace our human lowliness through the Incarnation of the Eternal Word. Mary's praise rebounds strongly with these themes:

> He has shown the strength of his arm
>> he has scattered the proud in the thoughts of their hearts.
>
> He has brought down the powerful from their thrones
>> and lifted up the lowly;
>
> He has filled the hungry with good things
>> and sent the rich away empty.   (Luke 1:51-52)

The thrust of Cardinal Newman's ministry as a Catholic priest echoed these promises of the Lord and brought their comfort to thousands. In this he is a shining example to every priest today. He highlights the priorities of the ministry of a priest and demonstrates with great clarity that personal ambition, even exceptional personal giftedness, should never draw a priest away from ministry to the people in his care.

In the summer of 1864, Bishop Ullathorne held a Synod of the Clergy of the Diocese of Birmingham. In the course of that meeting, an address to John Henry Newman was given on behalf of his fellow clergy. Newman was surely not wrong when, in the *Post scriptum* of the *Apologia pro vita sua*, he described this address as an "extraordinary honour".

In this address, the clergy of the Diocese paid tribute to Newman's courage and eloquence in defending himself against "a false and unprovoked accusation." But they also thank him for vindicating the honour of the Catholic priesthood. Addressing him "as a neighbour and colleague" they "express veneration and affection for one whose fidelity to the dictates of conscience, in the use of the highest intellectual gifts, has won even from opponents unbounded admiration and respect."

Given the circumstances that Newman had faced, this much is not surprising. What is more impressive is what follows. The priests of the Diocese indicate how close they are to him, and how much help and support they have received from him in their own ministry.

"To most of us you are personally known. Of some, indeed, you were, in years long past, the trusted guide, to whom they owe more than can be expressed in words." And so they continue: "We rejoice in numbering among our brethren one so well qualified by learning and experience … and we esteem ourselves happy in being able to offer you that support and encouragement which the assurance of our unfeigned admiration and regard may be able to give you under your present trials and future labours."

Priests are notoriously slow in offering public praise to one of their number. But here they do so. Such praise was most certainly well-earned.

In that same *Post scriptum*, Newman also printed in full a letter from Dr Ullathorne. He describes it as "a most gracious testimonial" and with Bishop Ullathorne's agreement "transfers it to his own document."

Dr Ullathorne's letter spells out the extent and nature of Newman's pastoral ministry. His knowledge of this ministry went back over nineteen years, and he had been Bishop of Birmingham for sixteen of those years. His testimony, alongside that of the clergy, is most significant.

In writing, Bishop Ullathorne's first concern was to dispel any misapprehension or 'erroneous impression' that during his years as a Catholic priest Newman had been more occupied with his own thoughts than with the service of religion and the work of the Church.

In contrast to any such view, Bishop Ullathorne went to great trouble to detail all that Newman had contributed. First he recalled the written productions which his Catholic pen had given to the world, making a formidable list of all those writings and noting that they represented but a portion of his labour.

He then spoke of the founding of the Congregation of the Oratory, both in London and Birmingham, moving on to the work Newman undertook with regard to the founding of the University in Ireland. More relevantly to this reflection, Ullathorne noted that in all these undertakings Newman never laid aside or suspended his parochial responsibilities.

We learn more of Newman's exercise of these responsibilities not only from this letter of Bishop Ullathorne but also from the centenary sermon preached by Fr Vincent Blehl, Postulator of the Cause of Cardinal Newman on 21 February 1990 in the Birmingham Oratory. That sermon is included in this volume, but I will also use it here.

Newman's pastoral work can be considered under the three principal duties given to a Catholic priest at his ordination. He is to celebrate the sacraments, preach the Gospel and exercise the care of souls, 'in the person' of Christ, the Head of the Church. This is what Newman did, and in an exemplary fashion.

Fr Blehl tells us of Newman's devotion to the celebration of Mass and to the Sacrament of Reconciliation from his first days in the converted gin factory in Alcester Street, which had become the first Oratory. This tradition still continues in St Anne's, Alcester Street. After many changes it is now the responsibility of the Order of Mary Immaculate, the OMIs, to say Mass, hear confessions and proclaim the Word of God in that place. I'm sure that they and many other priests draw inspiration from Cardinal Newman.

The Oratory in Alcester Street also founded two schools, clearly part of that desire to proclaim and teach the Gospel. After moving to Edgbaston, the Oratorians, under Newman's leadership, established poor schools for the same purpose. Then it was the turn of Smethwick, for there, too, the mission and the school owe their origin to Newman and his fellow Oratorians.

Preaching, the celebrations of Mass, time spent in the confessional, all occupied the time of these priests and their example is still hugely important. Not only were they regular in these duties, they were also ready to help other clergy in Birmingham who were under strain themselves. Indeed, Bishop Ullathorne noted that when the cholera epidemic hit Bilston and the two priests of the town were no longer equal to the task, Fr Newman and Fr St John themselves chose to respond to Ullathorne's request for additional help from the Oratorians. Furthermore, as he wrote, "they remained in Bilston till the worst was over".

In fact the most outstanding aspect of Newman's pastoral work in Birmingham was his work among the poor. Newman not only admired the devotedness of the Birmingham clergy to the poor but he excelled in it himself. His work in a Birmingham gaol is well recorded. His regular visiting of the sick and the poor was accompanied by practical help: getting jobs for the unemployed, giving coal to the poor and paying for medicines for the sick. Surely the visits to the elderly of Fr Newman were as welcome as those of any priest, if not more so. An outstanding example of this practical pastoral care was his visit to the Cadbury chocolate factory to plead that the Catholic employees should not lose their job even though they were refusing to attend the daily Bible instructions.

One more aspect of Newman's pastoral ministry in Birmingham is worthy of note. During the last twenty-five years of his life at Edgbaston there was a constant stream of visitors from all quarters and walks of life. Many came to seek the guidance of this remarkable priest. Indeed there were thousands who were in his spiritual debt, for he was a perceptive guide, having himself made his own remarkable journey.

Fr Blehl gives us quotations from key people which are wonderfully illustrative of Newman's work as guide and pastor. The *Birmingham Post* summed him up in this way: "Men thought he was the servant of the unseen and eternal powers, and when they came near him it was easier for them to believe in God and in God's nearness to mankind." A Protestant writer added that Newman was a "Roman cardinal in title but the light and guide of a multitude of grateful hearts outside his own communion and beyond the limits of these small islands." A true pastor indeed, one who had time, who made time, for all who sought his help.

Testimony to the greatness of Cardinal Newman's pastoral work in Birmingham came at the time of his death in August 1890. Newman's body was laid out in the Oratory church and hundreds came to pay their last respects and to pray. *The Daily Mail* wrote: "These visitors to the church comprised almost every class and every age, from venerable gentleman of affluence to the butcher boy with his basket on his arm." For the Funeral Mass an estimated 20,000 people lined the streets as his body was taken the eight mile journey to Rednal where he was buried. Many of the houses passed en route had black drapes hanging from their windows.

The testimony of the people about their priest is usually not far from the mark. It is usually given with charity and magnanimity during the priest's life. But at his death a more heartfelt voice can be heard. There would appear to be no doubt that Fr John Henry Newman was a much loved and holy priest for his people. He brought to them the grace and compassion of Christ in a manner that was loving and practical. He opened for them a glimpse of the promise of heaven which enabled them to live their faith more readily. In their turn they gave him their love.

At the recent installation of Pope Benedict XVI an innovation was introduced into the ceremony. Instead of the entire College of Cardinals coming forward to offer their respect and obedience to the new Pope, a group of twelve people were chosen. They included three Cardinals and then others from different states and walks of life within the Church. Among them was a parish priest. As that priest met the new Pope, and as they talked together, at ease and with real warmth, I was struck by the significance of the moment. It is often said that for most Catholics the two figures who most define their faith and shape its expression are their parish priest and their Pope. Here they were together in a moment of wonderful affirmation for parish priests everywhere.

Now I cannot restrain my imagination. If by some change of time, Cardinal Newman could have been part of that ceremony, bringing about a meeting between Pope Benedict XVI and himself, where in that group would he have been? Most, I expect, would like to see him there among the Cardinals. For my part, I would have liked to see him there as the parish priest. Then, I think, the depth of his holiness of life would shine forth most clearly.

Archbishop Vincent Nichols of Birmingham in Rome beside a poster welcoming Pope Benedict XVI, 23 April 2005.

Photograph by Peter Jennings

Abbot Cuthbert Johnson OSB, of Quarr Abbey, Isle of Wight, presented Pope Benedict XVI with
a copy of the *Rule of St Benedict*, specially bound in white leather in the bookbindery at Quarr,
following the Pope's General Audience in St Peter's Square on Wednesday 6 July 2005.

Fotografia Felici

Shared values:

Newman, Guéranger and Benedict XVI

Abbot Cuthbert Johnson OSB

On Thursday 11 July 1833 a young French priest, Prosper Guéranger, restored monastic life to France after its destruction at the French Revolution, by founding a small Benedictine community in the hitherto deserted Priory of Solesmes: a turning point in the life of the young priest Guéranger and an important moment for the history of the Church in France.

On the following Sunday the young John Henry Newman, on hearing a sermon preached by John Keble in Oxford, reached a turning point in his life and an important moment for the history of the Church in England. In his *Apologia* Newman wrote: "Sunday, 14 July, Mr Keble preached the Assize Sermon in the University Pulpit. I have ever considered and kept the day, as the start of the religious movement of 1833".

The seeds of the Oxford Movement were sown and Newman began the first steps towards his conversion to Catholicism. And this in not just the same year, nor the same month, but only three days after Prosper Guéranger sowed the seeds of what would lead to a European monastic revival stemming from the restored priory of Solesmes.

These two great men – Newman, who has been called a pioneer and prophet of the Second Vatican Council, and Guéranger, whom Pope Paul VI described as the "Father of the Liturgical Movement" – met each other in the Birmingham Oratory in September 1860 and shared their ideas about their common area of interest: Tradition and the writings of the Fathers of the Church.

The revival of interest in the study of the Liturgy and the writings of the Fathers of the Church, which Guéranger initiated in France and Newman promoted in England, was not an isolated phenomenon. In Germany there was a similar re-awakening in the appreciation of the values of the role of the Liturgy in the life of the Church and the Patristic tradition. In Germany in 1832 Johann Adam Möhler, Professor at Tübingen and Munich, published his controversial work *Symbolik*, which was to have a far reaching influence in promoting liturgical studies.

A few years earlier one of Möhler's first works was described as heralding "a rejuvenescence of the Church and of theological science". Like Newman, and obviously like Guéranger, Möhler had a love for St Benedict and two years before his death began preparing a history of monasticism, with the intention of setting forth the immeasurable influence of the Benedictine Order on Western civilization. Unfortunately his untimely death meant that this work was never completed. Three streams of thought, each one with a Benedictine aspect, each with a liturgical dimension and each rooted in the solid doctrine and teaching of the Fathers of the Church.

The work begun by Newman, Guéranger and the German school of Theology was to develop and lay the foundations for the work of the Second Vatican Council.

It has not been sufficiently emphasised that the Second Vatican Council took place at a time when the Church was enriched and spiritually blessed by the scholarship of religious, clergy and members of the laity. Experts in many disciplines and areas of theology were available in a measure which is sadly not the case today.

Among the advisors at the Second Vatican Council was the young Professor Joseph Ratzinger, who in those years gained experience of the universal Church in the persons of the bishops of the local Churches gathered in Rome. Cardinal Bernardin Gantin of Benin, who was created a cardinal by Pope Paul VI together with Joseph Ratzinger in 1977, stated recently: "He is a man who was nourished by the Second Vatican Council and a man who knows the Tradition, and who knows the Fathers of the Church." (*Avvenire,* 27 April 2005).

Both from the name he chose on his election and his known reverence for Saint Benedict, Joseph Ratzinger, now Benedict XVI, shares not only in the academic values of Newman, Guéranger and Möhler, but also in their understanding of the important formative role of the rule of St Benedict in the history and culture of Europe.

It would not be a surprise if the sentiments expressed by Cardinal Newman regarding the Benedictines found an echo in the sentiments of Pope Benedict XVI. In reply to an address presented to him at the Birmingham Oratory on 18 September 1879 from the Congregation of English Benedictines, Newman said: "The Holy Church at all times, early and late, is fair and gracious, replete with winning beauty and transcendent majesty: and one time cannot be pronounced more excellent than another; but I from a boy have been drawn in my affections to her first age beyond other ages, and to the monastic rule as it was then exemplified; and how was it possible to drink in the spirit of early Christianity, and to be enamoured of its loveliness, and to sit at the feet of the Saints, Anthony, Basil, Martin, Jerome, Paulinus, Augustine, and others, without a special sensibility and attraction to the grandeur of St Benedict, who completes the list of ancient monastic Saints, or without a devout attachment to his multitudinous family?

> And when I became a Catholic, and found myself a son and servant of St Philip, I rejoiced to think how much there was in the substance and spirit of his Institute, like that which I had attributed to the primitive monks. His children, indeed, have no place in the pages of ecclesiastical history. We have not poured ourselves over Christendom century after century; have not withstood a flood of barbarism, and, after its calamities, 'renewed the face of the earth;' we take up no great room in libraries, nor live in biographies and in the minds and hearts of spiritual men; but, as children of a Saint, we cannot but have a character of our own and a holy vocation; and, viewing it in itself, we may without blame ascribe to it a likeness to a Benedictine life, and claim a brotherhood with that old Benedictine world; in the spirit of Cardinal Baronius, one of St Philip's first disciples, who tells us in his *Annals,* that by and in St Philip's rule a beautiful apostolic method of spiritual life was

renewed, and primitive times came back again. There are none, then, whose praise is more welcome to me than that of Benedictines; but it need scarcely be said, my dear Fathers, that to have a vivid admiration of a rule of life is not the same thing as to exemplify it. I know myself better than you do; you think far too well of me, and I beg your good prayers that I may be more like that ideal of work and prayer which in your charitableness you identify with me.

Pope Benedict XVI sees the monk and abbot St Benedict as constituting a fundamental point of reference for the unity of Europe and a strong reminder of the inalienable Christian roots of its culture and its civilization.

Pope Benedict concluded his discourse with the words:"We know the recommendation left to his monks in his Rule by this Father of Western monasticism: 'Prefer absolutely nothing to Christ' (Rule 72:11; cf. 4:21). At the beginning of my service as Successor of Peter, I pray to St Benedict to help us to hold firm the centrality of Christ in our life. May he always be first in our thoughts and in all our activity!"

Dom Laurence Shepherd, Chaplain to the Nuns at Stanbrook Abbey and a friend of Guéranger, paid the following tribute to the Abbot of Solesmes shortly after his death in 1875:

> The Abbot, Dom Guéranger was perhaps the most learned Prelate of his age, at least in those sciences which are ecclesiastical. God had gifted him with all those talents which are requisite for a Master in Christian Israel. He wrote much, and not a single error can be detected in his writings. His whole life was a life of study and prayer; and what he once read, he never forgot, and could use it, years after, when occasion served. In every line, he reveals his burning love for the Church. This love for the Church might be called his ruling passion. It was his very life. He knew its spirit, its history, its traditions.

It will at once be evident that the description of Guéranger could equally be applied to the Venerable John Henry Cardinal Newman; it could also be applied to describe Pope Benedict XVI. And it could be added that, like Cardinal John Henry Newman, who was by nature rather reserved, the Pope is also somewhat reserved, a quality which is linked to his evident humility and exquisite courtesy.

Cardinal Newman c. 1883.

Courtesy of the Fathers of the Birmingham Oratory

Part five

History of the Newman Cause

Cardinal Newman
Rednall
July 22. 1881

Courtesy of the Fathers of the Birmingham Oratory

Decree on Heroic Virtues of the
Servant of God John Henry Newman

22 January 1991

The Decree of the Congregation for the Causes of Saints concerning the cause for canonization of the Servant of God John Henry Newman, Cardinal of the Holy Roman Church, and founder of the Oratory of Saint Philip Neri in England.

On the question: "Whether it is certain that he practiced the theological virtues of Faith, Hope and Charity towards God and his neighbour, and the cardinal virtues of Prudence, Justice, Temperance, Fortitude and those connected with them, in a heroic degree, in accordance with the requirements of the investigation of this case".

"Everyone who is of the Truth hears my voice" (Jn 18:37). The cultivation and love of the truth, who is Christ Himself, was like a brightly-burning lamp which lit the way for the Servant of God, John Henry Newman. Guided by this light in the exalted and saving knowledge of divine mysteries, he was directed towards the perfect imitation of Jesus Christ, the supreme model of perfection, and towards the zealous service of God's people.

Born in London on 21 February 1801, the son of John Newman and Jemima Fourdrinier, he was reborn to divine life in baptism, which he received in the Church of England on 9 April of the same year. He has left his own account of those events of his youth, which he describes as a "spiritual conversion", addressing God thus: "Thou didst change my heart, and in part my whole mental complexion at that time". These few words embrace and sketch out the exceptional character of the life of the Servant of God, as a man intent on finding God who is Truth, and therefore as attentive to His voice.

As a result of these youthful experiences he made a resolution whose principal elements were daily mental prayer and meditation on Holy Scripture, as well as careful self-examination and penance. He remained constant in this aim even while he was an undergraduate at Oxford, and later still as a fellow of the prestigious Oriel College. Growing ever more aware that he was called to a single life in the service of his neighbour, he embraced celibacy with a generous spirit. He was ordained deacon in the Church of England in 1824, and Minister in 1825; while on both occasions he became conscious of a more urgent call of service to souls. It was a call he was to put into practice throughout his life.

Soon after his ordination he was entrusted with the church of St Clement in Oxford, and showed himself unusually zealous in his parochial ministry, taking good care to visit each and every home and family.

He was appointed vicar of the University Church of St Mary the Virgin in 1828, and soon afterwards he began a serious study of the Fathers of the Church. This source of doctrine, together with his inner experiences while travelling in Sicily, led him not to choose his own way, but to allow God's Will to lead him on.

Returning to England, he was now certain that God intended to entrust some divine task to him. He believed that this task was to defend the Church from "Liberalism", which the Servant of God defined as the principle that no certain, objective truth exists in religion. It follows from this principle that one religion is as good as another; and therefore all religions should be tolerated, on the grounds that dogma is only based on opinion.

From 1833 to 1845 he wrote many works in defence of the Church. In these he was so determined and vigorous that he was unavoidably plunged into controversy. His uprightness and consideration towards those with whom he argued were remarkable, as was his love of truth. His books, his many exchanges of letters, his sermons and his devoted pastoral care, all ensured that his spiritual influence extended far beyond the bounds of Oxford.

His study of the Fathers of the Church now led him to begin to have doubts about the Church of England. From 1839, when this began to happen, and for the next six years he constantly sought the light, not only by study, but also by prayer and fasting.

During this time of questioning he suffered many anxieties; particularly the fear of causing sorrow to his family, the inability of his friends to understand, and the injustices to which he was publicly subjected. Nevertheless, he continued his line of enquiry. His study of the development of doctrine convinced him that what the followers of the Reformed Church tradition described as "Roman corruptions" were in fact true developments in the understanding of Revelation, and that the Catholic Church and the Church of the Fathers were one and the same. As soon as he realised that he must enter that Church, he was received into the Church of Rome by Blessed Dominic Barberi on 9 October 1845.

After his transition to the Catholic Church, John Henry Newman spent a long time in meditation, prayer and study, giving himself up entirely to seeking God's Will. This led him to priestly ordination in Rome on 30 May 1847. Through sound spiritual discernment he chose to follow the way of the Congregation of the Oratory of St Philip Neri, and was given permission to found the Birmingham Oratory.

There he was to spend the remainder of his life as a parish priest, thoroughly devoted to the service of the poor. Joining the Catholic Church brought both labours and suffering; but, as he later revealed, it was the presence of Christ in the Blessed Sacrament that was his mainstay and consolation at that time.

Eager to advance the intellectual education of Catholics, he accepted the post of Rector in the Catholic University of Dublin. When he and all Roman clergy were attacked in 1864, he proved himself a faithful defender of truth, publishing in reply his famous book, *Apologia pro vita sua*, or Defence of his life.

As a priest fired with the desire to save souls, his vast correspondence gave light and assistance to many Catholics and non-Catholics who turned to him with their doubts and difficulties.

As a faithful servant of Christ and his bride, the Church, he defended the definition of papal infallibility by the First Vatican Council, in the well-known Letter to the Duke of

Norfolk. Pope Leo XIII esteemed him so highly on account of his brilliance and learning that he raised him to the rank of Cardinal in 1879.

Consequently he was regarded with honour and esteem in his own country. Nonetheless he continued to live a life of great simplicity, completely dedicated to the pastoral care of all those who sought him out at the Birmingham Oratory. When he became almost totally blind, and was therefore unable to read any longer, he would constantly pray the Rosary, which he called one of the most beautiful of all prayers. He faced his approaching death with a peaceful and steadfast spirit as a good soldier of Christ, dying at Birmingham on 11 August 1890.

His body was laid out in church and a great number of persons of every class and creed came to honour him, and to pay their respects to one who had been a shining example to them, as well as an exceptional pastor. John Henry Newman's theological thought is of such stature and profundity that he is judged by many learned men to rank alongside the greatest Fathers of the Church.

But besides his intellectual achievement, his lifelong and fruitful ministry was marked by all the characteristics of a true pastor, one whose priestly charity moved him to direct his attention to the poor, whom he would help in whatever way he could. He came to the assistance of all who turned to him with their cares, as well as many of his fellow-countrymen throughout the land who were in need of comfort and advice.

These are the two outstanding features of his religion and of his devotion. In him they are perfectly combined by reason of his unique love and affection, which led him to become a man of faith and prayer. His many written works bear witness to this, particularly certain hymns and prayers that are even now a part of the spiritual and liturgical patrimony both of the Catholic Church and of the Church of England.

His way of life commands our admiration in its straightforwardness and frugality, totally founded on the Lord who is present in the Holy Eucharist and in the hearts of believers. He was wholly directed by the Spirit of the Lord who shaped him in the likeness of his Divine Master, meek and humble of heart, rich in forgiveness and gentleness towards the poor and lowly, and those in need of God's mercy.

On account of these qualities the Servant of God and his message are of great significance for our time and have enormous bearing on the modern world.

His reputation for holiness, strong enough while he lived, grew even greater after his death. Therefore the Archbishop of Birmingham inaugurated the cause for his canonization, establishing the Ordinary Informative Process between 1958 and 1986, whose judgement was recognised by the Congregation for the Causes of the Saints on 20 February 1989. After the *Positio,* or Case for his holiness, had been drawn up, a meeting of the Historical Consultors was held on 12 December 1989; and a special meeting on the subject of Newman's virtues was held on 20 April 1990, under the chairmanship of the Promoter of the Faith, the Most Reverend Antonio Petti.

Then on 8 January 1991, the cardinals and bishops assembled in Ordinary Congregation declared, in response to the Case presented by His Eminence Cardinal Giuseppe Caprio, that the Servant of God John Henry Newman had practised the theological, cardinal and other virtues to a heroic degree.

When the Cardinal Prefect of the Congregation for the Causes of Saints, Cardinal

Felici, had given a correct and faithful account of this case to the Sovereign Pontiff, Pope John Paul II, His Holiness ordered that the decision of the Congregation concerning the heroic virtues of the Servant of God, which he accepted and ratified, should be published.

When this had been done, the Holy Father summoned the Cardinals, the Prefect, the Proposer of the Cause, the Secretary to the Congregation and all the others who are usually invited to attend. Then in their presence the Holy Father solemnly declared that:

> It is certain that the Servant of God, John Henry Newman, Cardinal of the Holy Roman Church, Founder of the Oratory of St Philip Neri in England, had practised the theological virtues of Faith, Hope and Charity towards God and his neighbour, also the cardinal virtues of Prudence, Justice, Temperance and Fortitude and those connected with them, to a heroic degree, in accordance with the requirements of the investigation of this case.

The Sovereign Pontiff then ordered that this decree be published, and entered among the "acta" of the Congregation for the Causes of the Saints.

Given at Rome, 22 January 1991
Angelo Cardinal Felici, Prefect
Edward Nowak, Titular Archbishop of Luni, Secretary

John Henry Newman and Ambrose St John at the Propaganda College in Rome, 1847 by Maria Giberne.

Courtesy of the Fathers of the Birmingham Oratory

Newman and the Miraculous Medal

The picture by Maria Giberne (1802-85), long-time friend of the Newman family and convert to Catholicism in 1846, is especially interesting because the artist has placed in the background the shadowy figure of Our Lady of the Miraculous Medal. Newman's connections with the Miraculous Medal were significant. Newman was given a Miraculous Medal by George Tickell, a friend who had became a Catholic in 1844 and came to visit him at Littlemore and was later to become a Jesuit.

Newman was being prayed for in France especially by Father Dufriche Desgenettes at Notre Dame des Victoires in Paris. He had formed an association that had an image of the Miraculous Medal as its badge. Newman acknowledged the success of this prayer by a visit to the shrine on 11 September 1846 as he was making his way to Rome with Ambrose St John.

In his letter to Edward Pusey (1800-82) of 22 August 1867, Newman tells him that the date is significant because it was on 22 August 1845, three months before his conversion, that he put on the Miraculous Medal. Our Lady of the Miraculous Medal appeared to a Jew, Alphonse Ratisbonne, (1814-84), on 20 January 1842, who was converted to Catholicism by the experience. He became a priest. His brother had already become a priest, and was Deputy Director of the Shrine of Our Lady of Victories, though it is not known whether Newman met him.

When Newman and Ambrose St John (1815-75) arrived in Rome they found that their windows at the Propaganda College looked down directly on the church of San Andrea delle Fratte, where Our Lady had appeared to Alphonse Ratisbonne. Ambrose's room looked directly into the chapel where Our Lady of the Miraculous Medal had appeared.

Fr Gregory Winterton

Fr Paul Chavasse, Provost of the Birmingham Oratory, holding a copy of the first edition of the *Apologia*, standing at the desk at which Newman wrote it in 1864.

Photograph by Peter Jennings

Cause for the Canonization of
John Henry Cardinal Newman

Fr Paul Chavasse, Postulator of the Newman Cause

To examine the history of the Causes of the saints is to enter into one of the byways of history. We meet there all sorts and conditions of men and women; great intellects and humble folk; founders of orders, institutes and schools, and quiet souls who never stirred much from hearth and home.

The late Pope, John Paul II, was responsible for canonizing and beatifying the largest numbers of saints ever. Some of the causes that reached fruition in his Pontificate had been on the way for a very long time, not a few from the Middle Ages and from the centuries of religious upheaval in Europe. Others, most notably St Padre Pio, Blessed Teresa of Calcutta and St José Maria Escriva, died very recently and had their causes completed in relatively short periods. It is difficult, therefore, to predict in any given case quite how long it will take to reach the longed-for moment of a ceremony of beatification or canonization. It is easy to say, but it is nonetheless true: these things rest, firstly in the hands of God, and secondly in the hands of the faithful, as they pray and work for the glorification of a particular servant of God and for a miracle of physical healing through his or her intercession.

Which brings us to the Cause for John Henry Cardinal Newman. Surely, people argue, a man of such eminent learning and holiness, a man whose life and writings have influenced not only individual believers, but the whole Church, surely such a one should by now be beatified at the very least? After all, they say, 115 years have elapsed since he died; why the delay, when others who died much more recently are already honoured by the Church?

Newman died on 11 August 1890; many were the tributes paid to him then, and not a few of them spoke of the holiness of his life and the likelihood that one day he would be proclaimed as a saint of the Catholic Church. This quotation from *The Cork Examiner* for 18 August is typical: "Cardinal Newman goes to his grave with the singular honour of being by all creeds and classes acknowledged as the just man made perfect … even today all Catholics revere him as a saint." If someone today had fifteen hundred obituaries written about the sanctity of their life, one could imagine that their Cause would be introduced immediately. That this did not happen after Cardinal Newman's death is the result of several factors combining together: the Oratorian spirit of reticence, of wishing to be unknown, made Newman's own community reluctant to push the matter; the Modernist crisis in the Church in the years following the Cardinal's death and the suspicion some had of his writings in this respect; the political upheavals of the First World War – all this resulted in a delay in anything happening to pursue Newman as a candidate for canonization.

The first tentative move was made forty-five years after the Cardinal's death, in 1935

– just seventy years ago. This was not in England, but in Canada, where the Archbishop of Toronto, George McGuigan, issued the first prayer cards promoting the Cause. Some six years later the New York-based Jesuit journal *America* published in its edition of 22 November 1941 a letter, written by Fr Charles Callan, calling for Newman's canonization and for him to be made a Doctor of the Church. For several months after this the magazine carried letters supporting the idea. The correspondents were seeking to promote not so much Newman as the Cardinal, or even a man of prayer, but a man who had grappled with the demands of faith and intellectual honesty in a way which struck a chord with the experiences of so many in the middle of the twentieth century.

As the Second World War ended, so the Church in England, prompted by Pope Pius XII himself (who wrote an important letter about it)[1] celebrated the centenary of Cardinal Newman's reception into the Catholic Church. To mark the event the French Oratorian, Fr Louis Bouyer, wrote an article for the *Dublin Review*, entitled 'Newman's Influence in France'[2]. In it he said: "I would venture to say that what attracts us to him is what cannot be expressed by any other title than that of the Saint of our times…." This article, and the book that grew from it (*Newman: His life and spirituality*)[3], which was published in 1952, turned out to be pivotal in the history of the Cause. The book came to the attention of Fr H Francis Davis, a professor of theology at Oscott College, the Birmingham Archdiocesan seminary. In a subsequent article, Davis himself affirmed Newman's sanctity and urged the introduction of his Cause. The Fathers of the Birmingham Oratory sent copies of the article to English-speaking bishops, and having received encouraging replies, passed a formal decree on 28 February 1955, empowering Fr Philip Lynch (1891–1989), the then Superior, to request Archbishop Grimshaw of Birmingham to introduce the Cause.

So, just fifty years ago, the first steps, albeit hesitating ones, were finally being taken. One result of the 1955 decision was that Fr Stephen Dessain (1907–1976) of the Birmingham Oratory began his great (and, at the time of writing, still unfinished) labour of editing and publishing Cardinal Newman's massive archive of letters and diaries, with the object of using this largely untapped resource as an aid to proving the holiness of the writer. The first volume of the series appeared in 1961; it is hoped the thirty-second and last will appear in 2007.

The Archbishop of Birmingham did not formally introduce the Cause until June 1958 and it was not until October 1959 that the four historical commissioners were appointed to begin the work of investigating the Cardinal's life and writings. It must be admitted that these early years were not outstandingly successful. Some evidence was gathered together and witnesses interviewed – perhaps most importantly, Fr Denis Sheil (1865–1962), the last surviving Birmingham Oratorian who had known Newman personally. Prayer cards were printed and distributed to help foster interest and devotion, and various international contacts were made. So matters rested when the Second Vatican Council opened in the autumn of 1962.

The Council gave the Cause something of a boost. During one of the sessions, Pope

---

[1] Pope Pius XII, *The Service of Truth,* 12 April 1945. Latin original in Acta Apostolicae Sedis XXXVII, 1945, pp. 184-186.

[2] Louis Bouyer, *Newman's Influence in France*, Dublin Review 435 (October 1945), pp. 182-188.

[3] Louis Bouyer, *Newman sa vie, sa spiritualité*, Paris: Editions du Cerf, 1952. English translation: *Newman, his life and spirituality,* London, Burns & Oates, 1958.

Paul VI beatified Fr Dominic Barberi, the Passionist priest who had received Newman into the Church in 1845. It was an opportunity seized upon by the Pope to talk about the significance of Newman, whose writings were referred to on several occasions during the Council's debates. In 1964 a group of bishops attending the Council signed a petition calling on the Pope to beatify Newman forthwith as a benefit to the whole Church. In the turbulent years after the Council, the process of editing and publishing the Letters and Diaries continued steadily, but the Cause itself languished.

In 1973 Pope Paul asked for information about the state of the Newman Cause, in the hope that he might be able to beatify the Cardinal during the Holy Year of 1975, but it soon became apparent that much more work had to be done before this could happen. Documentary evidence had still to be collected, papers and books examined, and devotion increased. This last was greatly aided in two ways. Firstly, by "The Work", (now "The Spiritual Family The Work"), who organised the Academic Symposium in Rome in 1975, which attracted much interest from the Vatican. Among others, the Prefect of the Congregation of the Clergy, Cardinal Wright, and the Prefect of the Congregation for the Causes of Saints, Cardinal Raimundi, strongly encouraged The Work to continue with their commitment to Newman. The Centre of Newman Friends was set up, based in Rome. Later, when branches in other countries were founded, it became known as the International Centre of Newman Friends. Secondly, in October 1976, the Birmingham Oratory founded a society known as the Friends of Cardinal Newman. Father Stephen Dessain had announced its launch early in the year, but after his sudden death at the end of May, Father Gregory Winterton took it on. Under his guidance, this international Society has done sterling work, in increasing knowledge of, and devotion to, the great English Cardinal. Both Newman Societies have closely co-operated ever since.

The election of Pope John Paul II in October 1978 brought into the highest prominence someone who had long been interested in Newman's Cause, and who understood its significance for the whole Church. May 1979 saw the centenary of Newman being made a Cardinal, and the Pope sent a message to Archbishop Dwyer of Birmingham, in which he expressed his personal interest in the Cause and his hopes that it might soon reach a happy conclusion. This renewed interest from Rome acted as a stimulus to a somewhat reluctant Archbishop, and in late 1979 a new Historical Commission was set up, headed by Fr Vincent Blehl S J, of Fordham University, a long-standing friend of the Birmingham Oratory and a well-respected Newman scholar. Vincent Blehl was assisted by Fr Derek Holmes, an English Church historian, and by Gerard Tracey, the Archivist of the Birmingham Oratory, whose knowledge of Newman was as encyclopaedic as it was legendary.

This stage of the Cause's history, although done largely out of the public eye, was nevertheless absolutely crucial. The Commission, when it began its work in 1980, had to examine Newman's own writings (some 90 volumes) for their spiritual and theological significance, and also had to research the letters, memoirs, autobiographies and biographies of his friends, associates and enemies. The letters written to or about Newman in his own lifetime numbered between 50,000 and 70,000. In addition, the Commission had to collect secondary material in the shape of newspaper and magazine articles, biographies of Newman and their reviews. Finally, they had to sort through some 80,000 letters about

Newman, written after his death to his literary executor, to the Oratory, or to the vice-postulators of the Cause, for evidence of Newman's holiness of life.

The advent of new Papal legislation about Causes in 1983 and the appointment of Maurice Couve de Murville, an ardent supporter of the Cause, as Archbishop of Birmingham, led to the reconstituting of the Commission and the setting up of the newly-required Diocesan Tribunal to take testimonies regarding Newman's reputation for holiness.

By May 1986, the Historical Commission had completed its vast work and was able to submit 6,483 pages on Newman's life, virtues and reputation for holiness to the Diocesan Tribunal. The following month all the material was sent to the Congregation for the Causes of Saints in Rome. In July of the same year Fr Vincent Blehl was appointed Postulator of the Cause and immediately began work on the next, crucial, stage.

For every candidate for beatification and canonization there has to be written a sort of spiritual biography, known as the *Positio super virtutibus*, which is an abridgment of the findings of the Commission. Its findings have to be presented in a specific way, according to the virtues which adorn the Christian's life, so that the Congregation for Saints, its advisors and consultors, and ultimately the Pope himself, can judge whether indeed a case had been presented to show that the candidate, in this case Cardinal Newman, is worthy of canonization. For any candidate this is not an easy task; in the case of Cardinal Newman it was particularly difficult: trying to present this complex character in a way required by the Roman authorities, but also in a manner which would preserve something of the originality of the man, the engagingly human Cardinal, with his inimitable style and outlook.

Fr Blehl completed the two large volumes that comprise the *Positio* in 1989, and it was duly submitted to the Congregation for the Causes of Saints. When the present writer was participating in the course for new Postulators in Rome in the spring of 2003, it was gratifying to have Fr Blehl's work held up as one of the best examples of recent *Positios*, both for the scholarship it enshrines, as well as for the clarity of its writing.

The *Positio* portrays very clearly the spiritual greatness of John Henry Newman. What comes across to the reader is Newman's humility in the face of so many trials; his deep faith and trust in God and, of particular importance, his dedication to the spiritual ideals of the Oratory – for this was accomplished in the privacy of the Oratory and shows Newman living his priestly life in faith, hope and love. Even more importantly, the *Positio* reveals Cardinal Newman as always living in the presence of God, and as someone who had a great reputation for holiness. This became apparent from the evidence contained in the thousands of letters the Historical Commission had examined. The spiritual influence he exercised during his lifetime, and has continued to exert ever since, is so great that it must be regarded as an ongoing moral miracle.

It is worthwhile quoting Fr Blehl's conclusions: "Newman combined within himself what might seem contradictory traits not usually found in the same individual. What emerges is a spiritual portrait showing Newman as a man totally dedicated to God, to the Church, and to his fellow beings; a kind, lovable, thoughtful, strong yet gentle person, who preached and pursued the ideal of holiness as the end and purpose of life. In light of this harmony, one can conclude that he practised not one or two but all the virtues to an heroic degree."[4]

In the summer of 1989 the *Positio* was submitted to the Congregation for the Causes of Saints. The arguments it presented were so persuasive that it passed though all the various stages with remarkable rapidity – indeed, it was perhaps the fastest ever at that time. So it was that on 22 January 1991, Pope John Paul II was able to declare that John Henry Newman had indeed lived out the virtues to an heroic degree and was a suitable candidate for beatification and canonization. He was therefore accorded the title "Venerable" – that is, worthy of veneration.

The Cause had reached a milestone and had done so, all things considered, relatively quickly. One suspects that such rapidity led some people to conclude that the next stage would also be completed equally quickly. Unfortunately, this was not to be the case.

The next stage, that leading to beatification, required the proving of a miracle of physical healing ascribed to Cardinal Newman's intercession. Obviously, this is something that it is impossible to predict as it depends upon the prayer of the faithful for sick people and upon God's response. Whilst one can encourage the first, one cannot legislate for the second. As was said at the beginning of this essay: this is an important lesson – after all the work and scholarship of examining a candidate's life and virtues are over, the 'making of saints' rests solely in the hands of God.

Helping our fellow Church members to trust in Cardinal Newman as their heavenly friend and intercessor is now the work of all those who wish to see him declared a saint. People do turn to him in increasing numbers, and the Postulator's Office in Birmingham regularly receives reports of cures and healings of one sort or another, as well as the more ordinary favours, concerned with such things as jobs found, houses sold, exams passed and the like. Reports of medical cures are examined closely to see whether or not a particular case might prove to be the miraculous intervention that is needed. Several have seemed hopeful – a lady cured from persistent ulcers; a teenage boy haemorrhaging to death and whose bleeding suddenly stopped; a man cured overnight of a huge brain tumour. For one reason or another, whether confusion over what prayers were said and to whom, lack of cooperation from medical staff, missing documentary evidence from doctors and hospitals, these cases have had to be put on one side. The marshalling of witnesses and the presentation in meticulous fashion of the necessary documents has to be done to the highest level of accuracy possible, so as to rule out any accusations of slipshod approaches or special pleading. This is only right when one is dealing with such supremely important matters.

It is the belief of those working for the Postulator that it is only a matter of time before a case arrives which meets all the necessary requirements. Given the interest in the Cause in Rome (from Popes John Paul II and Benedict XVI down), when something does happen, it is easy to imagine that things will reach a conclusion very quickly. This would serve to fulfil the hopes of the late Pontiff, John Paul II, who wrote in his letter of 2 January 2001, marking the 200th anniversary of Cardinal Newman's birth:

---

[4] Citation from Vincent Ferrer Blehl SJ (ed.), Birmingham, Cause of Canonization of the Servant of God, John Henry Newman (1801-1890), Founder of the English Oratories; *Positio super virtutibus* (Rome, 1989) 2 volumes, Congregation of the Causes of Saints 1238 (Birmingham, V F Blehl SJ: The Oratory, 1989) II, p. 53.

"(As) we thank God for the gift of the Venerable John Henry Newman ... we pray that this sure and eloquent guide in our perplexity will also become for us in all our needs a powerful intercessor before the throne of grace. Let us pray that the time will soon come when the Church can officially and publicly proclaim the exemplary holiness of Cardinal John Henry Newman, one of the most distinguished and versatile champions of English spirituality."[5]

Cardinal John Henry Newman c. 1883, photographed by H J Whitlock. Joseph Whitlock was the first professional photographer to work in Birmingham, setting up his studio at 120 New Street in 1842. His son Henry Joseph took over the business, moving to 11 New Street in 1864, where he photographed Newman.

Courtesy of the Fathers of the Birmingham Oratory

[5] Pope John Paul II, Letter to Archbishop Vincent Nichols, 22 January 2001.

Prayer for the
Beatification and Canonization
of the Venerable John Henry Newman

Eternal Father, you led JOHN HENRY NEWMAN to follow the kindly light of Truth, and he obediently responded to your heavenly calls at any cost. As writer, preacher, counsellor and educator, as pastor, Oratorian, and servant of the poor he laboured to build up your Kingdom.

Grant that through your Vicar on earth we may hear the words,

> Well done, thou good and faithful servant, enter into
> the company of the canonized saints.

May you manifest your servant's power of intercession by even extraordinary answers to the prayers of the faithful throughout the world. We pray particularly for our intentions in his name and in the name of Jesus Christ your Son our Lord.

Amen

Enquiries to:

The Postulator, Newman Cause, The Oratory, 141 Hagley Road,
Edgbaston, Birmingham B16 8UE

Tel: +44 (0) 121 454 0496   *Fax:* +44 (0) 121 455 8160

e-mail: oratory@globalnet.co.uk

Pope Leo XIII created Newman a Cardinal on 15 May 1879. Elected
Pope on 20 February 1878, Leo XIII died in Rome on 20 July 1903.

Courtesy of the Fathers of the Birmingham Oratory

Part six

Newman's Cardinalate

and the English Oratory

San Giorgio in Velabro by Emmeline Dean, 1881.

A watercolour painting of San Giorgio in Velabro, Cardinal Newman's titular church in Rome, by Emmeline Dean, hangs in his room at the Birmingham Oratory.

Courtesy of the Fathers of the Birmingham Oratory

Letter from Pope John Paul II to

George Patrick Dwyer, Archbishop of Birmingham

In spiritual communion and with pastoral solicitude I gladly respond to your invitation to celebrate together with the Church throughout England the centenary of the elevation to the Cardinalate of one of her great sons and witnesses of the faith, John Henry Newman, created Cardinal of the Holy Roman Church by my venerable predecessor Leo XIII on 12 May 1879, with the title of St George in Velabro.

The elevation of Newman to the Cardinalate, like his conversion to the Catholic Church, is an event that transcends the simple historical fact, as well as the importance it had for his own country. The two events have long since been deeply inscribed in ecclesial life far beyond the shores of England. The providential meaning and importance of these events for the Church at large have been seen more clearly in the course of our own century. Newman himself, with almost prophetic vision, was convinced that he was working and suffering for the defence and affirmation of the cause of religion and of the Church, not only in his own time but also in the future. His inspiring influence as a great teacher of the faith and as a spiritual guide is being ever more clearly perceived in our own day, as was pointed out by Paul VI in his address to the Cardinal Newman Academic Symposium during the Holy Year 1975: "He [Newman] who was convinced of being faithful throughout his life, with all his heart devoted to the light of truth, today becomes an ever brighter beacon for all who are seeking an informed orientation and sure guidance amid the uncertainties of the modern world – a world which he himself prophetically foresaw." (Address of 7 April 1975).

In raising John Henry Newman to the Cardinalate, Leo XIII wished to defend and honour his activity and mission in the Church. Acceding to the earnest desire expressed by members of the English laity under the leadership of the Duke of Norfolk, the Pope meant to pay tribute to the genius of Newman and to give public expression to his own personal appreciation of Newman's merits. He intended to recognize the value of Newman's many writings in defence of God and the Church. In this way Pope Leo upheld and encouraged all those – inside and outside the Catholic Church – who regarded Newman as their spiritual teacher and guide in the way of holiness. Newman himself made this comment on the Pope's intentions: "He judged it would give pleasure to English Catholics, and even to Protestant England, if I received some mark of his favour" (Talk given on his reception of the Biglietto, 12 May 1879). The philosophical and theological thought and the spirituality of Cardinal Newman, so deeply rooted in and enriched by Sacred Scripture and the teachings of the Fathers, still retain their particular originality and value. As a leading figure of the Oxford Movement, and later as a promoter of authentic renewal in the Catholic Church, Newman is seen to have a special ecumenical vocation not only for his own country but also for the whole Church. By insisting "that the Church must be prepared for converts, as well as converts prepared for the Church" (J.H. Newman, *Autobiographical Writings* (ed. H Tristram)), he already in a certain measure anticipated in his broad theological vision one of the main aims and orientations of the Second Vatican Council and the Church in the post-conciliar period. In the spirit of my predecessors in the See of Peter, I express the hope that under this very important aspect, and under other aspects no less important, the figure and teaching of the great Cardinal will continue to inspire an ever more effective fulfilment of the Church's mission in the modern world, and that it will help to renew the spiritual life of her members and hasten the restoration of unity among all Christians.

It is my hope that this centenary will be for all of us an opportunity for studying more closely the inspiring thought of Newman's genius, which speaks to us of deep intellectual honesty, fidelity to conscience and grace, piety and priestly zeal, devotion to Christ's Church and love of her doctrine, unconditional trust in divine providence and absolute obedience to the will of God.

I also wish to express my personal interest in the process for beatification of this "good and faithful servant" (cf. Mt 25: 21) of Christ and the Church. I shall follow with close attention whatever progress may be made in this regard.

In extolling his memory and his contribution to the Church of God I send my special Apostolic Blessing to you and to all the faithful of England, and in particular to the members of the English Congregation of the Oratory of St Philip Neri, of which John Henry Newman was the founder, as well as to all those who revere him throughout the world.

From the Vatican
7 April 1979
Signed John Paul II

150th Anniversary of the

Foundation of the English Oratory

Homily by Bishop Philip Boyce OCD
The Birmingham Oratory, 2 February 1998

Today's Feast, the Presentation of the Lord, is a joint commemoration of Christ, the Son of God, and of his Blessed Mother. It celebrates a mystery of salvation accomplished by Christ – his first entrance into the Temple in Jerusalem to meet his people. In this mystery Our Lady was closely associated with her Son, as the Mother of the Suffering Servant of Yahweh who came to the Temple to be offered.

Mary, the Mother, appears in this mystery as a splendid pattern for all followers of her Son, who in their pilgrimage of faith "are ever being tested in their faith and hope through suffering and persecution". And all of us, with lighted candles in our hands, go out to meet the Lord, to welcome him as the *Lumen Gentium,* the light of the nations, renewing our resolve to live as children of the light and to spread the light of Christ's Gospel by our words, our works and our entire way of life. "But the chief importance of this event consists in its being a fulfilment of prophecy" as John Henry Newman once said in an Anglican Sermon for this very feast day. We have just heard the prophecy of Malachi proclaimed: "The Lord you are seeking will suddenly enter his Temple." (Malachi 3:1). We commemorate in faith the first accomplishment of that prophecy, as it took place forty days after the birth of Christ.

The sermon to which I referred was entitled the Secrecy and Suddenness of Divine Visitations and was preached on 2 February 1831. In the course of it, Newman stated that any such liturgical celebration "may, for what we know, be wonderfully connected with some ancient purpose of his, announced before we were born, and may have its determinate bearing on our eternal welfare." (*Parochial and Plain Sermons* II, p. 115). He could not have imagined then, young and confident curate that he was, that seventeen years later to the day he would, with Solemn First Vespers of this Feast, admit the first nine members and thereby set up the Congregation of the Oratory of St Philip Neri in England. He thus became its Founder and Father. It was a moment of grace, a "divine visitation" that would have a salutary influence on the lives of many people. From it would spring a spiritual family that would play a significant role in the ecclesiastical history of this country.

When Newman meditated on the mystery of this Feast of the Presentation, he was struck by the silent but sure ways of divine Providence which brings to fulfilment God's designs in circumstances that are simple and unnoticed by the multitude. Referring to the scene in the Temple at the Presentation, he quotes another prophet Haggai: "The glory of this latter House shall be greater than the former" (2:9). "Behold the glory," he comments, "a little child and his parents, two aged persons, and a congregation without name or memorial. 'The kingdom of God cometh not with observation'" (*Parochial and Plain Sermons* II, p. 110).

We could say much the same about those Solemn Vespers at Maryvale where it all took place: "Behold the glory; Father Newman with five Fathers, one Novice and three Lay Brothers. A simple ceremony unheralded and unheeded by the public at large". Yet, today, the members of the various Houses of the Oratory, with friends from near and far, recall with gratitude those humble beginnings and celebrate with due solemnity the sesquicentennial of the Foundation of the Oratory in England. Newman's dreams have in many ways found their fulfilment in his spiritual sons and in the history of these one hundred and fifty years.

In the foundation Brief (departing somewhat from the formal and impersonal tone of a Papal Brief), Pope Pius IX stated that he had looked forward with firm and joyful expectation to the time when he could "establish and authorise a society of men, outstanding in learning and holiness, who would themselves be Englishmen" for the purpose of "consolidating the Catholic Religion in the powerful and thriving Kingdom of England" (cf. *Newman the Oratorian,* Dublin, 1969 p.422). After fervent prayer for this intention, Newman's request for approval of the foundation of the Oratory of St Philip Neri in England seemed to him to be the desired grace. "There is no need to say how pleased we were at this proposal: *Quantopere Nobis hoc initum a Joanne Henrico Newmanio propositum placuerit … magis clara res est, quam ut eam oporteat verbis explicare."* (ibid., pp. 423, 425). Very few Papal Briefs came to Founders of Societies of consecrated persons with such personal warmth and the Pope saying, in effect: "It is just the Foundation I have been waiting and praying for!"

The ideal however, like all approved Rules of Perfection, is a demanding one. Newman had a thorough grasp of the Oratorian vocation and the spirit of St Philip Neri. He adapted it marvellously well to the English scene of the nineteenth century, while retaining all that was essential. St Philip Neri was renowned, Pius IX said, because he had "devoted his whole life to the salvation of souls" and because in all his apostolic ministry he had been "the father in Christ of countless persons." (ibid. p. 426). As Newman once said in his youth: "Holiness is the great aim". A Father of the Oratory, he later said, lives in community as a secular priest, and as such he "has the duties of a secular priest, and is bound to aim at perfection in the exercise of those duties" (ibid. p. 344). He has to be completely dedicated to the cause of Christ and be a spiritual father of many souls.

To arrive at their ideal, Newman the Founder illustrated in his Chapter Addresses some of the spiritual and human qualities the Fathers would need. For example, their zeal for souls and holy life would be personified "in men of *gentlemanlike manners and refined feelings."* (ibid., p. 189). He is speaking of the Christian gentleman, in whom refinement of mind is not cultivated for its own sake, but is "superadded to a high religious perfection". The Oratory training enables a man to wield personal influence through the goodness and nobleness of his life, to act for himself in a responsible way, and yet to perform his duties in unison with other members of a united body or community. By complementing each other, the whole body gains in spiritual vigour and ability.

Hence community and residence are all-important. A son of Philip Neri must learn to be at home in his room or nido, serve the Lord with joy and find his maxima mortificatio in the demands of community life. Learned studies and literary pursuits belong to the spirit of the Oratory, but they too must be "directed solely to the glory of God and the salvation of souls, which are the ends of the Christian ministry." (*ibid*. p. 323).

Let us not forget the place of the Virgin Mary in the example and spirit left by Cardinal Newman to his Oratorian sons. Jean Guitton called him the Doctor Marianus of the nineteenth century. The biblical and Patristic foundation of his teaching on Our Lady gives it considerable ecumenical value. So too does his somewhat original contribution of highlighting the difference between Marian doctrine which is constant and solid and Marian devotion with its ebb and flow and its changing cultural expressions. Newman's own theological and doctrinal exposition of Marian truths was sober and scientific, but he also knew the warmth of devotion and admiration. He for whom the Church Fathers were enough (cf. *Difficulties of Anglicans* II, 24-25), also fingered his beads until his dying days in his favourite prayer, the Rosary, and two months before his Reception in 1845 he began to wear a miraculous medal (cf. *Letters and Diaries of John Henry Newman* XXIII, 318). Preaching on the fourth anniversary of the establishment of the Oratory in England (1852), he said that this Feastday of the Purification (as it was then called) was "a great day" for the Congregation, and he added: "To me [it is] especially interesting, for it has been my great feast-day for thirty years. Thirty years this year since I was brought under the shadow of our Lady (elected Fellow of Oriel, the House or Hall of Blessed Mary), whom I ever wished to love and honour more and more." (*Sermon Notes of John Henry Cardinal Newman, 1849-1878*, (London, 1913), pp. 102-103). His veneration for Mary was not simply intellectual theory; it descended into practical living. He changed the name of the College buildings, offered to him by Bishop Wiseman, from Old Oscott to Maryvale, a name that remains to the present day. He chose the title *Sedes Sapientiae* for Mary as Patroness of the Catholic University in Dublin. For him, Mary, pondering the word of God, excelled the greatest of theologians in her knowledge of things divine (cf. *Meditations and Devotions* (London, 1893), p. 34). To all of you, his spiritual sons, he would say as he used to say to correspondents: "Put yourself ever fully and utterly into Mary's hands and she will ... bring you forward." (*Letters and Diaries of John Henry Newman*, XIV, 29).

I offer in conclusion my warmest congratulations to all the Fathers and Brothers of the Oratories here today. I thank them for having transmitted and remained faithful to the rich heritage left to us all; but to them in a particular way, by Cardinal Newman. I thank them for having offered a haven of peace, for many who like Newman himself came "into port after a rough sea" (*Apologia pro vita sua*, p. 238). And our common thanks goes to the Father, the giver of all good gifts, on this 150th anniversary of the establishment of the Oratory in England. All the sons of St Philip Neri have abundant cause for thankfulness to him. To conclude, let us make our own the words of Newman himself in an Address to his own Community in 1854:

> For myself, when I look back eight or nine years, and bring before
> my memory the changes that took place in my life, how little could
> I fancy that in the course of so short a time I should find myself in a
> house like this [Hagley Road], so truly a home in every sense of the

word, spiritual and temporal! How little had I reason to expect, except that the word of promise was sure, that by giving up I should so soon receive back, and by losing I should gain! And what is true of me, is true of you too, my dear Fathers and Brothers, of each in his own way.

(*Newman the Oratorian,* p. 290).

Bishop Philip Boyce DD, OCD, of Raphoe (Ireland) in Newman's Room at the Oratory House, Edgbaston, on 2 February 1998. He received a doctorate in theology in 1977 with a dissertation on the Spirituality of Cardinal John Henry Newman.

Courtesy of the Fathers of the Birmingham Oratory

Part seven

Celebrations of two Centenaries

in Birmingham

Newman's birth 1801

Newman's death 1890

Newman lecturing at the Corn Exchange, Birmingham,
by Maria Giberne, c. 1851.

Courtesy of the Fathers of the Birmingham Oratory

Newman delivered a series of lectures later published as *The Present Position
of Catholics* to meet the anti-catholic prejudice started up nationwide by the
appointment of the Catholic Hierarchy in 1850. The lectures, noted for
their satire, were officially delivered to the "Brothers of the Little Oratory"
but the picture shows at least one lady in a bonnet who managed, like the
artist, to get in to hear Newman speak.

Newman Centenary Celebrations
Birmingham 1990

Cardinal John Henry Newman, England's most famous nineteenth century churchman, died in his room at the Birmingham Oratory at about 8.45 pm on the evening of Monday, 11 August 1890. He was 89. At the time of his death newspapers and magazines in England published numerous articles and tributes about Newman. *The Times* wrote: "Whether Rome canonizes him or not, he will be canonized in the thoughts of pious people of many creeds in England."

Highlight of the worldwide 1990 Centenary Celebrations was a solemn sung Mass of the Holy Spirit, for the Beatification and Canonization of the Servant of God, John Henry Newman, at the Newman Memorial Church, situated next to Newman's Oratory House in Birmingham. The Provost, Fr Gregory Winterton, was the principal concelebrant and preacher at the Mass, celebrated by Fathers of the Birmingham and London Oratories, together with Provosts representing some of the other seventy Oratories throughout the world. The Apostolic Pro-Nuncio to Great Britain, Archbishop Luigi Barbarito and the Apostolic Nuncio to Ireland, Archbishop Emmanuel Gerada, were also present for the historic occasion.

Among the special guests at the Mass were Miles Fitzalan-Howard, 17th Duke of Norfolk, and the Duchess of Norfolk; John Broadley, the British Ambassador to the Holy See; and Councillor Bernard Zissman, the Lord Mayor of Birmingham. Also present were Mr and Mrs J O Mozley, Mr and Mrs Geoffrey Thomas, and Miss Miller (descendants of Newman's sister Jemima). (Newman's two sisters Harriet and Jemima married two brothers named Mozley). There were also representatives of places where Newman lived and worked both as a Catholic and an Anglican – Littlemore, Trinity and Oriel Colleges, Oxford, and Dublin – during his long and distinguished academic and pastoral life.

After a luncheon hosted by Fr Winterton, a short but deeply moving service of hymns, readings and prayers was held near Newman's graveside at the Oratory House, Rednal, on the outskirts of Birmingham. The sun glinted through the spreading trees in the peaceful Victorian garden as the Pro-Nuncio to Great Britain, Archbishop Luigi Barbarito, led everyone present in the special prayer for Newman's beatification and canonization. Archbishop Barbarito described Cardinal Newman as: "A great evangelizer and a man of deep spirituality." He continued: "Newman's relationship with God was so ordinary that people did not realize that he was always living in the presence of God. This is a good example for all of us." As the afternoon drew to a close, small groups stood in silent prayer in the simple community graveyard, where Newman is buried in the same grave as his great Oratorian friend, Fr Ambrose St John.

Such is the worldwide interest in Cardinal Newman that the Visitors' Books in his study-chapel at the Oratory House started during the 1950s reveal that visitors from more than 125 countries have come to see where he exercised his great apostolate. In the cloister leading to his Memorial Church, consecrated on 23 June 1920, there are tablets on the wall to the memory of the departed Oratory Fathers. On the tablet bearing Newman's name and coat of arms is the simple Latin inscription: "*Ex umbris et imaginibus in veritatem*" ("Out of shadows and images into the truth").

A small committee, working under the direction of Fr Gregory Winterton, masterminded the programme of successful Centenary events in Birmingham. Fittingly, the official celebrations began in Newman's Memorial church on Wednesday 21 February 1990, the anniversary of Newman's birth in 1801, with a special Mass in honour of St Valentine, a Roman martyr whose mortal remains lie in the Oratory church. The saint's body was found in the catacombs and given to Fr Newman by Pope Pius IX when he left Rome in 1847 with authority to set up the Congregation of the Oratory in England.

Cardinal Basil Hume, OSB, Archbishop of Westminster, President of the Bishops' Conference of England and Wales, was the chief concelebrant together with many of the bishops of England and Wales, who had been present in St Chad's Cathedral, earlier in the day, for the Episcopal Ordination of Canon Philip Pargeter, as the new Auxiliary Bishop of Birmingham. Fr Vincent Blehl S J, Postulator of the Newman Cause, who wore the red chasuble given to Newman when he was made a cardinal in 1879, preached the sermon, on 'Newman and Birmingham'. The vestment bears Newman's coat of arms and motto *Cor ad Cor loquitur* (Heart Speaks to Heart). It was a memorable occasion and the church looked magnificent with flowers and candles adorning the sanctuary and all the side chapels.

Newman was closely associated with St Chad's Cathedral, situated in the centre of Birmingham, where he preached a course of Lenten sermons in 1848, and the sermon at the installation of Bishop William Bernard Ullathorne OSB, the first Catholic Bishop of Birmingham.

A special performance of *The Dream of Gerontius* was given in Birmingham Town Hall, on the evening of 23 June 1990 by the City of Birmingham Symphony Orchestra and the City of Birmingham Choir, conducted by Christopher Robinson. The English composer, Sir Edward Elgar, set Newman's great poem to music for the Birmingham Music Festival 1900, and it was first performed in Birmingham Town Hall. The manuscript of Elgar's score, re-bound and restored during the 1980s, is kept at the Birmingham Oratory.

In London a national Ecumenical Service was held in St Paul's Cathedral, on Friday 23 November 1990, to honour Cardinal Newman, who made a profound and lasting impression on both the Anglican and Catholic Churches of his day. The Archbishop of Canterbury, Dr Robert Runcie, and the Archbishop of Westminster, Cardinal Basil Hume OSB, led the service.

At the time of his death in August 1890, *Freeman's Journal,* an Irish Catholic newspaper, wrote on 20 August 1890, the day after Newman's funeral: "No peer, or prince, or priest, or merchant who ever walked the crowded streets of Birmingham is so missed or mourned as the Roman Cardinal."

Fr Blehl suggested that the reason why so many other celebrations had been planned for the Centenary Year could be found in what was written in the *Evangelical Magazine* and why, on the Sunday after Newman's death, mention was made of him not just in Catholic churches, but in many Anglican and Nonconformist pulpits of England: "Newman was felt to be both a great Englishman and a great saint."

"The influence of our Founder, the Venerable John Henry Cardinal Newman (1801–1890), is now worldwide," emphasized Fr Gregory Winterton at the end of the Centenary Celebrations on 21 February 1991. He added: "We are completely confident that in God's good time he will be beatified, canonized, and made a Doctor of the Church, to give the Church's authority to his already great and increasing spiritual influence."

Newman's grave at the Oratory House, Rednal, 11 August 1990, the centenary of his death.

Courtesy of the Fathers of the Birmingham Oratory

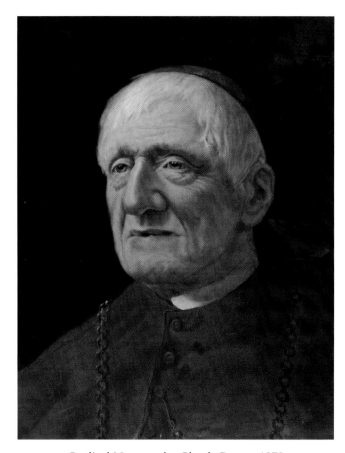

Cardinal Newman by Claude Pratt c. 1879.

Courtesy of the Fathers of the Birmingham Oratory

This striking portrait of Cardinal Newman was painted by Claude Pratt (1860–1935), a prominent Birmingham artist, during 1879–1880, after Newman was created a Cardinal by Pope Leo XIII. Newman received the red hat from Pope Leo during a ceremony in Rome on 15 May 1879. Pratt was still only 20 when the portrait was completed.

Born in Leicester in January 1860, Claude Pratt was not a Catholic when he first came to the Oratory in Edgbaston to meet his subject. He was converted to Roman Catholicism through coming to Mass and listening to the sermons preached by Cardinal Newman. Made a full member of the Royal Birmingham Society of Artists in 1888, he was elected honorary curator in 1925. He died on 24 September 1935.

The portrait, that hangs in the Oratory House, Birmingham, has not previously been published, except on the front cover of the privately circulated *Friends of Cardinal Newman Newsletter*, Christmas 2002.

Letter from Pope John Paul II
to Maurice Couve de Murville,
Archbishop of Birmingham

At the approach of the first Centenary of the death of John Henry Newman and in response to your kind invitation, I gladly associate myself with the celebrations that mark this event in England and indeed in many countries throughout the world. The memory of the great Cardinal's noble life and his copious writings seem to touch the minds and hearts of many people today with a freshness and relevance that has scarcely faded with the passing of a century.

The Centenary year coincides with the beginning of a period of profound change in world events. This period has begun with new prospects for genuine freedom and signs of a renewed awareness of the need to build life, both individual and social, on the solid foundation of unfailing respect for the human person and his inalienable God-given dignity. To all searching minds in this present historical context, Newman's voice speaks with a timely message.

Newman's long life shows him to have been an ardent disciple of truth. The unfolding of his career confirms the single-heartedness of his aims, as expressed in the following words that he made his own: "My desire hath been to have Truth for my chiefest friend, and no enemy but error" (*Via Media,* London 1911, Vol. 1, pp. xii-xiii). In periods of trial and suffering he persevered with confidence, knowing that time was on the side of truth.

Newman's quest for the truth led him to search for a voice that would speak to him with the authority of the living Christ. His example holds a lasting appeal for all sincere scholars and disciples of truth. He urges them to keep asking the deeper, more basic questions about the meaning of life and of all human history; not to be content with a partial response to the great mystery that is man himself; to have the intellectual honesty and moral courage to accept the light of truth, no matter what personal sacrifice it may involve. Above all, Newman is a magnificent guide for all those who perceive that the key, the focal point and the goal of all human history is to be found in Christ (cf. *Gaudium et Spes,* 10) and in union with him in that community of faith, hope and charity, which is his holy church, through which he communicates truth and grace to all (cf. *Lumen Gentium,* 8).

Closely connected with this call is John Henry Newman's teaching on the importance of conscience as a means to the acquisition of truth. His doctrine on conscience, like his teaching in general, is subtle and whole, and ought not to be oversimplified in its presentation. He sets out from the basic affirmation that conscience is not simply a sense of propriety, self-respect or good taste, formed by general culture, education and social customs. Rather is it the echo of God's voice within the heart of man, the pulse of the divine law beating within each person as a standard of right and wrong, with an unquestionable authority.

The inner light of conscience puts a person in contact with the reality of a personal God. In one of his books he wrote: "My nature feels towards the voice of conscience as towards a person. When I obey it, I feel a satisfaction; when I disobey, a soreness — just like that which I feel in pleasing or offending some revered friend ... An echo implies a voice; a voice a speaker. That speaker I love and revere." (*Callista* (London, 1910), pp. 314-315).

Moreover, according to Newman, religious obedience to this inner voice puts a person on the lookout for a divine revelation, leads from light to light and ultimately to Christian faith. "Obedience to conscience leads to obedience to the Gospel, which, instead of being something different altogether, is but the completion and perfection of that religion which natural conscience teaches" (*Parochial and Plain Sermons* VIII (London, 1908), p. 202).

One of Cardinal Newman's lasting merits, in fact, is his struggle to make clear and uphold the vital principle that revealed religion, with its content of doctrine and morals, is the bearer of objective truths which can be known with certitude and assented to with joy and ease (cf. *Dei Verbum* 5). Few people championed the full rights of conscience as he did; few writers pleaded so persuasively on behalf of its authority and liberty; yet he never allowed any trace of subjectivism or relativism to taint his teaching.

For this reason he taught that although conscience is within the human heart before it receives any training, it is still the duty of a Christian to inform and educate it through the guidance of an authority, in order to bring it to maturity and perfection. Left to itself and disregarded, it can become a counterfeit of the sacred power it is, and turn into a kind of self-confidence and deference to a person's own subjective judgment. Newman's words are unequivocal and perennially valid: "Conscience has its rights because it has its duties." (*Difficulties felt by Anglicans* II (London, 1910), p. 250).

By following the light of his conscience, Newman made a journey of faith, which he described with force and clarity in his writings. After spending the first half of his life in generous service to the Church of England which he deeply loved, he spent the second half in the service of the Catholic Church, showing a like sincerity and unflinching loyalty. The thoughts and convictions which gave rise to his conversion found their roots and inspiration in the writings of the Fathers of the Church, which are the common patrimony of all Christians. I have often urged that Christians need to rediscover together their common heritage of faith, if we are to see the reintegration of Christ's followers in the unity for which he prayed. This is a process that can be remarkably furthered by attention to the work of Newman.

It was characteristic of him to be firmly faithful to the truth once gasped, while being always ready to develop and deepen his understanding of the deposit of faith. It might be added, moreover, that he combined fidelity to the truth with an attitude of respect and receptivity to the ideas and testimony of those with whom he disagreed. Both in his person and in his work, therefore, Cardinal Newman illuminates the ecumenical journey that we undertake in obedience to the will of Christ (cf. John 17:21). His life and witness furnish us today with a vital resource for understanding and carrying forward the ecumenical movement which has developed so richly in the century since his death.

It is my fervent hope that the present Centenary year will occasion in the minds of many people who thirst for truth and genuine freedom a renewed awareness of the lessons to be gained from the life and writings of this outstanding Englishman, priest and cardinal. A man of such consistent loyalty and sincerity could not fail to inspire and draw many others towards the ideal he faithfully served. Not all agreed with the momentous decisions he took, or with the religious principles he advocated, but all unfailingly testified to the spiritual influence his example wielded over others. Some called him their guide in the paths of holiness; others were swayed by the silent force of his humble and withdrawn ways; still others found comfort and peace in his simple exposition of truth; while all were struck by his life of constant prayer and study, and by his familiarity in faith with the "things that are above" (Col 3:1).

Down to the present day, Newman remains for many a point of reference in a troubled world. They look to him as a man of great natural talent who put every ounce of it at the service of God and the Church. His remarkable life, void of sham and ambition, but steeped in a prayerful communion with the unseen, while it remained alive to the problems of his age in Church and society, continues to inspire, to uplift and to enlighten.

May the Centenary celebrations issue in abundant grace and spiritual vigour for the Church in England, for your own Archdiocese and for the members of the English Congregation of the Oratory of St Philip Neri, founded by John Henry Newman.

Finally, I take the occasion to send my greetings and my Apostolic Blessing to all the Friends of Cardinal Newman throughout the world.

From the Vatican,
18 June 1990
Signed John Paul II

Cardinal Basil Hume OSB (1923-1999), Archbishop of Westminster and President of the Bishop's Conference of England and Wales, in the chapel in Newman's Room on 21 February 1990, at the start of the Newman Centenary Year. Cardinal Hume later signed this photograph on 23 May 1999 before he left Archbishop's House to go into hospital where he died on 17 June.

Photograph by Neils McGuinness

Tribute to Cardinal Newman

Cardinal Basil Hume OSB

21 February 1990

Speaking at the start of Mass in the Oratory Church, Edgbaston, Birmingham, on 21 February 1990, at the opening of celebrations to mark the centenary of the death of Cardinal John Henry Newman, on 11 August 1890, Cardinal Basil Hume OSB, Archbishop of Westminster, said:

> A century after the death of Cardinal Newman the echo of his voice has not faded. If anything it has gained strength. Some of Newman's insights, in particular his keen appreciation of the importance of the role of the laity in the Church and his conviction about religious freedom, had a profound influence on the thinking of the Second Vatican Council.
>
> Newman's life was a remarkable example of a man's ceaseless yearning and striving for God. From his Anglican roots to his last days as an Oratorian, he responded with generous resolve to the call of God. It is right that we should celebrate him in this centenary year, devote further study to his thought, and give thanks for his life and his extraordinary legacy.

Centenary service in St Paul's Cathedral, London, October 1990. Left to right: Fr Vincent Blehl S J, Postulator of the Newman Cause, Dr John Newton, Free Church President of Churches Together in England (the preacher of the day), Dr Robert Runcie, Archbishop of Canterbury, Cardinal Basil Hume OSB, Archbishop of Westminster, Fr Gregory Winterton, Provost of the Birmingham Oratory.

Courtesy of the Fathers of the Birmingham Oratory

Newman and Birmingham

Fr Vincent Blehl SJ

Postulator of the Newman Cause

A Centenary Sermon preached in the Church of the Birmingham Oratory,

21 February 1990

A hundred years ago this coming August an account appeared in the *Agnostic Journal* of a man and his wife visiting Birmingham and deciding to go to early mass at the Oratory to see one whom the narrator referred to as "Father Newman". It was about daybreak, but no day broke; it was so rainy, foggy, sleety, cold, and dark that once or twice on the mile-long walk they paused, debating whether to go on. Surely Fr Newman would never rise from his bed on such a morning, and they would see only one of his subordinates. To their delighted surprise he appeared and said the mass. As they were returning the man said to the lady author who accompanied them, a devout member of the Church of England: "How do you explain Fr Newman? What can have caused a great scholar, orator, genius, to abandon the prospect of a splendid career in your Church, and now, at over three score and ten to scorn the elements that he may say mass for a few Irish domestics?" "There is," she answered, "for me but one explanation: a glimpse of the supernatural world. Under that vision this world and its glories shrivel up."

The lady was of course correct as far as she went; Newman revealed a more specific explanation in his letters to personal friends, namely, his response to the call of conscience – conscience not so much as the moral sense, as arbiter of right and wrong, but rather conscience in its religious modality, the channel through which God reveals his will to the individual, and the individual is invited to respond in loving obedience to God. And it was also in answer to such a call that Newman settled in Birmingham, as a priest and Oratorian, first in a converted gin distillery in Alcester Street, and then here in Edgbaston so that he might be closer to the centre of the city and hence exercise greater influence upon it. Here he lived, devoting himself to the daily routine of a parish priest; saying mass, hearing confessions, visiting the sick, and carrying on an enormous correspondence in which he assisted persons of all denominations with their religious and spiritual difficulties.

So unobtrusively did Newman work that his opponents said he buried himself, and the myth of Newman the recluse was propagated. The *Leamington Chronicle* put its finger on the half-truth hidden in the myth, when it wrote: "He did not court public applause, and when he retired from public life he tried to hide himself and lived, in Birmingham, in the most humble way."

What he did hide pretty effectively was his discreet charities to the poor, but we have Fr Neville, his literary executor, as a witness, and also a living tradition in the city, that Newman tried to get jobs for the unemployed, that he gave coal to persons facing the winter without it, and that he paid for medicines for the sick. And the most familiar example, when the Catholic employees at Cadbury's chocolate factory were about to lose their jobs for refusing to attend daily bible instructions, Newman, though in his late eighties, went off in the slush and cold of winter to plead for them successfully. But it was not only the poor he assisted; it was anyone who requested help. The Chairman of the Committee for the Birmingham Music Festival of 1888 asked him to try and secure the Duke of Norfolk as the President of the Festival Committee. Not only did he do so, but he himself attended the morning performances on the 28, 29, and 31 August together with the Duke of Norfolk.

In the *Apologia* Newman wrote that he never set himself up as a leader in the Church of England; people came to him. So it was during the last twenty-five years of his life in Edgbaston. There was a constant stream of visitors to the Oratory where he was a most hospitable and gracious host. Many have left accounts of how deeply affected they were by their encounter with him. Lord Coleridge wrote after one of his visits: "The fascination of the man, personally, is far the greatest I ever felt. He never talks controversy ... you feel all the while that you are talking to a great and holy Christian." And Baron Anatole von Hügel, after his first meeting with Newman, said: "It makes one feel how it is worth while to be a saint." The *Birmingham Daily Post* summed it up when it wrote: "Men thought he was the servant of the unseen and eternal powers, and when they came near him it was easier for them to believe in God and in God's nearness to mankind."

It was not surprising therefore that upon his death in August 1890 there was such an outpouring of sympathy and mourning over the departure of one so greatly loved and to whom literally thousands were spiritually and otherwise so deeply indebted. One paper wrote: "No peer, or prince, or priest, or merchant who ever walked the crowded streets of Birmingham is so missed or mourned as the Roman Cardinal." Newman was laid out here in the church and hundreds came to view the remains, to pray, and some to touch religious objects to his body. The *Daily Mail* reported that: "These visitors to the church comprised almost every class and every age, from the venerable gentleman of affluence, to the butcher-boy with his basket on his arm." On the day of the funeral the area outside the Oratory was jammed with people. An estimated fifteen to twenty thousand persons lined the streets as the cortege wound its way to Rednal eight miles away, for a peaceful burial. Many of the houses passed en route had black drapes hanging from their windows.

No editorial or obituary, of which there were well over a hundred in the newspapers throughout he country, was able to do complete justice to the many facets of Newman's genius or to his rich and complex personality. Nor is any such assessment the purpose of this evening's celebration. Rather we are gathered here to thank God for the extraordinary gifts, intellectual and spiritual, which he conferred on his servant.

This day is traditionally celebrated in the Oratory church as the Feast of St Valentine, whose body rests here having been brought from the catacombs in Rome with the permission of Pope Pius IX in December 1847 when Newman returned to England. It is also the day on which Newman was born in 1801, destined, we believe, to make an outstanding contribution to the spiritual life of the Anglican, Catholic, and Nonconformist Churches. Even during his lifetime his spiritual influence was widely acknowledged. One Protestant writer called him a: "Roman cardinal in title, but the light and guide of multitudes of grateful hearts outside his own communion and beyond the limits of these small islands." That influence has never ceased and is so widespread that to us who pray and hope for his canonization – as we have been doing these past three days – it constitutes a special sign of divine approbation.

It is with gratitude that we acknowledge the presence of the Lord Mayor and other distinguished dignitaries at this evening's opening of the Newman Centenary Year celebrations. Newman believed that an Oratory should be an important part of the city in which it is located, "a sort of ecclesiastical corporation," he said, "in which the town takes interest and feels pride." He would be pleased that the Oratory has become just that in Birmingham, as your presence so eloquently attests. So too we look forward gratefully to the other celebrations that are planned for this year. These are being sponsored by a wide variety of persons and institutions. If we need assign a reason for this plethora of events, it would no doubt be along the lines of what the Evangelical Magazine wrote to explain why, on the Sunday after Newman's death, mention was made of him not just in Catholic churches but in most Anglican and in many of the Nonconformist pulpits of England: "Newman was felt to be both a great Englishman and a great saint."

Previously unpublished picture
of Dr Newman c. 1863.

Courtesy of the Fathers of the Birmingham Oratory

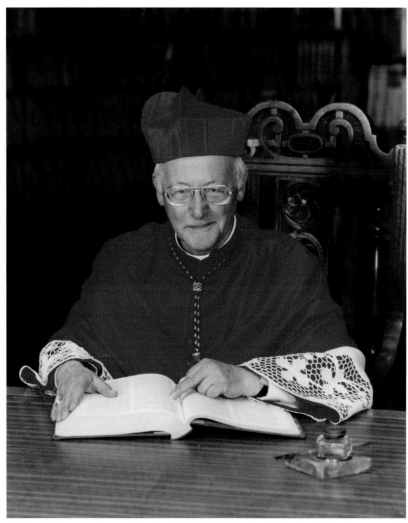

Cardinal Alfons Maria Stickler SDB, Archivist Emeritus of the Vatican Secret
Archives, in Newman's Library at the Oratory House, Birmingham, during a
visit for St Philip's Day, 26 May 1990.

Courtesy of the Fathers of the Birmingham Oratory

Newman and St Philip Neri

Cardinal Alfons Maria Stickler SDB

Sermon preached at the Church of the Birmingham Oratory
on St Philip's Day, Saturday, 26 May 1990.

My dear Brethren,

We are celebrating today the solemnity of St Philip Neri, in coincidence with the first centenary of the death of his greatest spiritual son, Cardinal John Henry Newman, and only five years from the fourth centenary of the saint's own return to God. We have excellent reasons, therefore, for reflecting on St Philip's life and his influence, both then and afterwards, on the whole Church.

There are three spheres in which his influence, direct and personal, or more generic and extensive, can be clearly seen. Firstly, let us consider the significance of the year of St Philip's birth, 1515: it was providential, in that it marked the beginning of a life of sanctity. But that was also the year in which Martin Luther's decision matured to reform the Church "in head and members". Of course, reform was long overdue! But Luther brought "deformation", rather than "reformation" to the Church and destroyed the centuries-old unity of Christendom. In one way or another the whole of Europe was affected – or afflicted – by what Luther set in motion. Some initial attempts at renewal of the Church's life also date to this crucial moment, but the real reform was achieved only through the General Council of Trent. Involved in the deliberations of the Council, and then in the implementation of its decrees, are a whole host of saintly men and women, many of whom are now formally canonized and raised to the honours of the altars.

A front-runner among them in Rome, at the very centre of Christianity, was Philip Neri, who became a focal point of the counter-Reformation. He was friend, advisor, and even confessor of Popes, Cardinals, Bishops and churchmen of every rank and influence. One needs only think of Ignatius of Loyola, Charles Borromeo, Francis de Sales, Camillus de Lellis, Felix of Cantalice – to mention only a few saints - and immediately one sees how Saint Philip's sanctity in Rome was reflected by them to the Universal Church.

The second sphere of St Philip's influence, that we should consider, is precisely his role as reformer of the Eternal City of Rome. He was the pioneer of new forms and methods of pastoral ministry, such as were called for by the changed times and mentality. But the success of his new approach can be explained only by his exceptional personality and character. He was a very humble man. He was absolutely simple and natural in his life-style. He was full of gladness and good humour, but with great sensitivity for the material and spiritual needs of others especially the poor and simple, and for their sufferings. He had an extraordinary capacity for friendship and was the perfect fulfillment of St Paul's maxim: "I have become all things to all men."

But it is the second part of this phrase from the Apostle's *Letter to the Corinthians* (1 Cor 9:22) that needs to be underlined, and that is, "that I may save them all". In all his social contacts, Philip Neri was motivated by one purpose – to communicate, to instruct, to enter into dialogue. To preach the truths and norms of Christian Life in the open as they processed from church to church, as they sang his popular hymns and took part in his attractive liturgical functions. His chief aim behind all this was to explain what prayer is, to make it attractive. To make penance, spiritual retreats, the frequent reception of the sacraments, especially Confession, attractive to the faithful.

Nor can we finish our reflection of this second sphere of St Philip's activity without saying a word about his special love for children. From the beginning of his stay in Rome and during those sixteen years as tutor to the children of his fellow Florentine Galeotto della Caccia, Philip Neri realised the importance of imparting a Christian education from earliest childhood. For the remainder of his long life of almost eighty years this was his favourite pastoral activity, to give children their first grounding in the Faith and in the practice of Christian Life, and in such an attractive and intelligent way, that this first instruction received from St Philip remained with them for the rest of their lives and they in turn became effective, indeed the most effective heralds of the Gospel and workers for religious renewal.

The third great quality of St Philip Neri which deserves our reflection, is a truly original charism from which the Universal Church has drawn benefit. From the outset Philip Neri recognised the need to work together, to collaborate no matter what the form of social or spiritual apostolate. Already in his first commitment to the numerous poor sick pilgrims, who thronged Rome, he had the idea of founding the Brotherhood of the Most Holy Trinity, who collaborated actively to meet their needs. He extended this form of pastoral "team-work" to the community of priests that he founded in the church of San Girolamo della Carita, specifically for priestly care of souls. This community, which the saintly founder called Oratorium, later moved to the church of Santa Maria in Vallicella. Pope Gregory XIII gave it his official approval and slowly it developed into a Congregation, which has constituted a real charism in the Catholic Church, namely, a community formed of secular priests (and later of laymen too, as collaborators) linked only by charity, but without vows, or promises. Each community is independent, autonomous, self-sufficient, and not dependent on any co-ordinating central organisation. This is all the more noteworthy in that, in the sixteenth century, in order to obtain recognition as a religious Order, every spiritual family had to profess public vows. Contemporary with the foundation of St Philip's Oratory were those other new forms of religious life, the so-called Clerics Regular – Camillians, Barnabites, Jesuits, Somaschians, Piarists, etc – all of whom tried to respond to the increasing demands of the apostolate in the ever wider world with a greater centralization of their organisation.

St Philip knowingly rejected all these forms of religious life. All he wanted was a community of secular priests working together for the care of souls under the jurisdiction of the local hierarchy. His charism became the model for those societies of common life without vows, which the new *Code of Canon Law* calls Societies of Apostolic Life. They differ, however, from Philip Neri's original charism in that they all have formal juridical ties albeit private ones, and, secondly, because they all depend from a more or less centralised organisation for their direction.

After St Philip's death numerous Oratories were founded along these charismatic lines, and so the saint's influence extended throughout the world to the Universal Church.

I cannot conclude this commemoration of St Philip Neri without devoting a few words to another aspect of this saint, one that is both surprising and encouraging: his relevance for our times. There is a greater crisis in the Church today than in that of Saint Philip's day. In many respects Europe today is dechristianised, hostile to the Faith, Godless! The authority of the Catholic Church is no longer accepted everywhere on every issue. Almighty God and His Divine Will have been replaced by human autonomy, the revealed Faith by human reasoning, the Commandments by the laws of our welfare society. With what good reason does our Holy Father, Pope John Paul II, insist continuously on the necessity of re-evangelising Europe. Our whole continent, and the others too, all have need of reformers such as St Philip in his day, and he can still serve as an excellent model for the apostles who must bring about the reformation needed today.

This apostolic renewal requires, as in Philip Neri's time, adequate new methods in order to reach the people successfully. From this point of view, St Philip's personality and the typical forms that his pastoral work took can and should serve as a model for today's evangelisation. A cheerful attractive mentality, open to dialogue, an awareness of the material needs and spiritual malaise that is so prevalent. A love of the poor, above all, of children and young people. A practical, simple method of instruction. And more than anything else personal conviction, such as St Philip radiated the need for prayer and the sacraments in our daily lives as Christians, with the immense benefits to be derived therefrom.

Finally we must emphasise the extraordinary actuality of St Philip's charism of working together as apostles, as reformers. In the present scarcity of priests and lack of vocations, all available forces must combine their efforts in order that their pastoral works be crowned with success in order to combat the deficiencies from which the Church suffers at the present moment.

Thus, communities of priests, not bound by special obligations, but like Philip Neri's Oratorians, could supply for the lack of pastors in the parishes already deprived of priests, but not remote from well located pastoral centres. Moreover, the brotherly support of community life could remedy the serious problems of isolation and loneliness which many priests suffer. A last consideration about the relevance of St Philip Neri. He received a solid philosophical and theological formation at the Sapienza University of Rome and from the Augustinians. He pursued his studies for the rest of his life, as his private library bears witness. Other highly competent churchmen asked for his opinion on disputed questions, although without doubt he preferred to be engaged in active pastoral work. Nevertheless, he retained a lifelong love for higher knowledge in all its forms and fostered this among his friends, his pupils and his spiritual sons. One thinks of the historical research and writings of Baronius; the efforts of Bosius exploring the undergound tunnels of the Roman Catacombs, where St Philip loved to meditate and pray; his interest in classical and church music, which his friend and spiritual disciple Giovanni Pierluigi da Palestrina brought to such a splendid height of perfection; his encouragement of the superb architecture of the Chiesa Nuova and the nearby Palazzo Borromini, with the rich and varied collections of the famous Vallicelliana Library. All this and many other things too testify to his love of art, culture and higher studies in every field.

Small wonder, therefore, that the newly-converted John Henry Newman, during the days of his preparation for the Priesthood, in Rome, in spite of his familiarity with eminent Jesuits, decided to join the Oratory of St Philip and found it in his native England. We can see in this great theologian a clear reflection of St Philip's charism, and one which continues to bear excellent fruits, through Newman's influence as a Doctor of the Church in the modern age, as the master of a true ecumenism, as a reformer of faith and morals that will bring about the real evangelisation of Europe.

Let us pray together in this Holy Sacrifice that such a saintly founder will continue to inspire his spiritual sons to live according to his charismatic example intensely, and also that Cardinal Newman may soon be recognised officially as a model to the whole Church of fidelity to vocation and mission.

St Philip Neri, by Guido Reni (1575-1642)
Santa Maria in Vallicella (Chiesa Nuova), Rome.

Courtesy of the Fathers of the Roman Oratory

Fr Gregory Winterton and Peter Jennings, beside Cardinal Newman's grave at the Oratory House, Rednal, on 11 August 1990.

Courtesy of the Fathers of the Birmingham Oratory

The Centenary of Newman's death

11 August 1990

Sermon given by Fr Gregory Winterton, Provost,

at the Church of the Birmingham Oratory.

On the evening of 9 August 1890 John Henry Newman, aged 89, returned to his room before retiring for the last time. His step was heard as he approached; it was not recognized as his. Entering his room he surprised his attendant because he was unbent, erect to the full height of what he was in his fifties, and without support of any kind. Fr Neville, his attendant who recorded the fact, made this significant comment: "his whole carriage was soldier-like; his voice was quite fresh and strong; his appearance was that of power, combined with complete calm."[1]

It should not surprise us that Newman faced death as a soldier. He had acted as one all his life. Filled with awe at the responsibility for souls that he was assuming in being ordained to the Anglican Ministry in 1824, he took courage in the thought, "I am Christ's soldier."

If Newman was a soldier, who were the enemies he was combatting? First, there was the spirit of liberalism in religion, which denied the objectivity of revealed truth and was undermining faith in the Christian revelation.[2]

Secondly, there was the easy-going, comfortable religion of the day which substituted an outward show of respectability for the authentic Christian life of self-denial and self-sacrifice. In a sermon, 'The World our Enemy'[3], Newman defined the world as those objects which, though essentially good, draw our affections away from God and centre them solely or mainly on ourselves: namely, money, prestige, comfort and pleasure. And what are the weapons that the soldier of Christ must use against this enemy?

They are, he said, the weapons of the Saints: humility, prayer, poverty, meekness, love of God and of the neighbour. And to this list we must add courage, for courage, even to the point of heroism, has always been the hallmark of great soldiers.

Those who knew Newman were struck by this element in his character. Principal Shairp said that one of his qualities as a leader was his "tamelessness of soul which was ready to essay the impossible." Newman's cousin Anne Mozley wrote that "the 'heroic' was a sort of natural element with him". In one of his most powerful sermons, 'Ventures of Faith,' he said: "Let everyone who hears me ask himself the question: what has he ventured for Christ?"[4]

---

[1] Meriol Trevor, *Light In Winter*, p. 644, quoting Fr William Neville.
[2] The *Biglietto* speech at the conferring of the Cardinal's hat in 1879.
[3] *Parochial and Plain Sermons* VI, sermon 3.
[4] *Parochial and Plain Sermons* VI, sermon 20.

And what of Newman's own ventures for Christ? We all know what they were. As a minister in the Anglican Church he worked tirelessly for his parishioners at St Clement's, St Mary's and Littlemore. He published volume after volume of sermons which reached thousands of persons beyond Oxford and awakened in them the desire for a stricter way of life and a greater union with God.

Becoming convinced that the Catholic Church was the one true fold of Christ, he sacrificed a fellowship at Oriel, a living at St Mary's, and he was ostracized by his relatives and friends when he joined a despised minority with whom he had little previous contact. A preacher, the Rev F Williams, speaking of this step affirmed that: "It showed a degree of heroism surpassing, in a sense, the sacrifice of the martyrs of God."

Nor as a Catholic did Newman cease "to essay the impossible." Bishops, heads of religious orders, and eminent and successful laymen in Ireland all told him that to plan the establishment of a Catholic university in Dublin was to attempt an impossibility. Yet he did establish it, because, as he said: "My sole aspiration is to be the servant of the Vicar of Christ, and he has sanctioned this undertaking." So too he began the Oratory School in Edgbaston, despite the many obstacles in the way of its success, in order to fulfil the special mission the Holy Father had given in the brief authorising the Oratory in England. He accepted the challenge of replying to Kingsley's attack on himself and the Catholic clergy by agreeing to publish a chapter of the *Apologia* every Thursday for seven weeks – a prodigious feat of endurance.

This determination of his did not go unrecognized. Thus it was that at his death editorials all over the country recognized Newman as a man of extraordinary talents, and they praised the many aspects of his career as controversialist, pastor, Oratorian, educationalist, writer and philosopher. They acknowledged that he had made a significant contribution to the spiritual life of the Anglican Church and was mainly responsible for destroying prejudice against Catholics in England. But there was also a general recognition of his marked holiness of life, his humility, his determination, his unworldliness and his singular integrity of character.

The recognition that Newman received at his death has now spread far and wide, so that today Newman is admired not only in England but all over the world. This is owing in no small measure to the researches of scholars, including past Fathers of the Oratory, who have collected and published the records of his life and thought. His influence on the Second Vatican Council is widely acknowledged, and he is regarded as a seminal and classic thinker who has inspired others in their search for truth. Thus it comes about that thousands of persons in different parts of the world are awaiting the official recognition by the Church, soon we hope to be pronounced by the Holy Father, that Newman was indeed a true soldier of Christ by reason of the heroicity of his virtues, and is therefore worthy to be called Venerable.[5]

And so we welcome and thank all of you who have come today, some even from far-off lands, to join us on this occasion, when we pay tribute to a truly great and courageous Christian and when we thank God for the example of his life and the benefits of his teaching.

---

[5] Newman was declared to have the virtues in a heroic degree on 22 January 1991.

I have a request to make. Recalling Newman's love and devotion to prayer and his lifelong conviction of its efficacy and power, I ask you one and all to pray for Newman's beatification, his canonization, and that he be declared a doctor of the Church. I also ask you to engage others in your own family, in your parishes, in your circle and country, to pray for a miraculous sign of God's approval from Heaven over and above the marvellous sign of his continuing and unending spiritual influence.

A popular writer once said Newman was a hero but not a saint. I hope that one day we may look upon him both as a hero and as a saint.

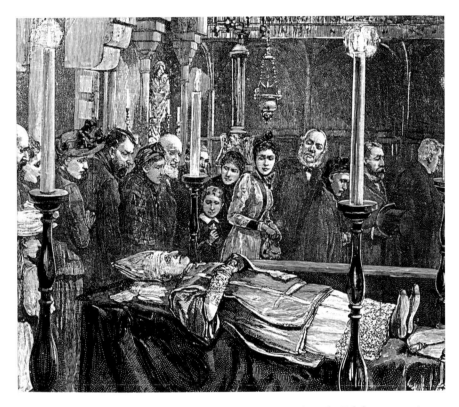

Cardinal Newman's lying in state in the Oratory Church, Edgbaston, prior to the Funeral Mass on 19 August, 1890.

Courtesy of the Fathers of the Birmingham Oratory

Archbishop, later Cardinal Edward Cassidy, President of the Council for Promoting Christian Unity, in Newman's room during a visit to the Birmingham Oratory in October 1990, with (left to right) Fr Gregory Winterton, Provost of the Birmingham Oratory, Archbishop Maurice Couve de Murville of Birmingham, and Fr Vincent Blehl S J, Postulator of the Newman Cause.

Courtesy of the Fathers of the Birmingham Oratory

Newman and the quest for Christian unity

Archbishop Edward Cassidy

Ecumenical service in St Anne's church,

Alcester Street, Birmingham, 30 October 1990

During this year in which we are celebrating the centenary of the death of John Henry Cardinal Newman, the question is often asked: how can Newman aid us in furthering and effectively achieving Christian Unity.

It might seem at first that the Newman experience is not one that can be of much help to those striving today to restore the unity of the *Una, Sancta, Catholica Ecclesia* of the first millennium – and in the West of the first millennium and a half. Was his not a lone journey from the faith of his baptism to membership of the Roman Church? Surely, we might think, such an experience could be invaluable for the individual who finds himself or herself in similar circumstances, but hardly a model for Churches who are striving to undertake the ecumenical journey together.

While there is of course some logic in this way of thinking, I am convinced that we have re-discovered in this year many aspects of Newman's journey of faith that illustrate essential aspects of our ecumenical journey and can be of significant assistance to us in furthering and making effective Christian Unity. It is I believe precisely some of these aspects of ecumenism that need to be stressed at this particular time if we are not to get bogged down in our endeavours.

As Pope John Paul II wrote in 1979 to Archbishop G P Dwyer of this Cathedral city of Birmingham: "Newman is seen to have a special ecumenical vocation, not only for his own country but also for the whole Church."

What then are the lessons that we can learn from this great nineteenth century man of the English Church? When Churches set out to seek unity, they first must get to know each other, to leave aside the prejudices and stereotypes that have bedevilled their past relationships and to replace them with respect and understanding.

The ecumenical rapprochement between Catholics and Anglicans in recent times has been made easier because of the change of attitude in public opinion in Britain towards the Church of Rome that occurred during the second part of the nineteenth century and continued through to the time of the Second Vatican Council. Newman's life and work made a significant contribution to this change, as even the *Belfast Morning News* admitted after his death, when it wrote that the Cardinal had: "wrought a gradual, almost imperceptible, change in the minds of Protestant Englishmen towards the body of their Catholic fellow-men. This, it would seem, was the most immediate and apparent result of his unblemished life. Cardinal Newman had made it impossible for Protestant Englishmen to dismiss the religion which he professed, as a farrago of absurdities and superstitions not worth examining. The prevalent opinion regarding Catholicism some thirty or forty years ago was that it was such a farrago, and it is mainly owing to the silent teaching and example of the great Cardinal who has gone that such a prejudiced view has been replaced by a saner and more common sense estimate."

In our ecumenical theological dialogue we are still striving to put into effect what was recommended by *Unitatis Redintegratio,* n.9, regarding the knowledge that we must achieve of one another's doctrine and life. On this point Newman wrote already in 1863: "Would that the Protestants know more of our doctrines! Then they would not find difficulties when there come really none in their way. On the other hand, I will say too: would that Catholics who have never been Protestants knew us better" (*Letters and Diaries of John Henry Newman* XX, 543).

The *Belfast Morning News* attributes Newman's influence on his fellow citizens to his unblemished life. How very important it is in fact that we give in our lives a true witness to our faith if we are to be effective ministers of ecumenism. How many of the divisions within Christianity have been deeply influenced by the failure of Christian men and women, especially of those with responsibility for leadership, to offer an authentic and credible witness of the faith they professed! Newman teaches us that we can further Christian unity only by living a coherent faith that witnesses to Christ's revealed truth and the demands of the Gospel. The Council Decree on Ecumenism, *Unitatis Redintegratio,* in n. 4, devotes considerable space to what is described as a primary duty of those who seek to contribute to the ecumenical ministry of the Church, namely: "An honest and careful appraisal of whatever needs to be renewed and achieved in the Catholic household itself, in order that its life may bear witness more loyally and luminously to the teachings and ordinances which have been handed down from Christ through the apostles".

Cardinal Newman summed up this requisite in the well-known phrase: "The Church must be prepared for converts, as well as converts for the Church." In the message already quoted from John Paul II to Archbishop Dwyer, we read: "The philosophical and theological thought and the spirituality of Cardinal Newman, so deeply rooted in and enriched by Sacred Scripture and the teaching of the Fathers, still retain their particular originality and value. As a leading figure of the Oxford Movement, and later as a promoter of authentic renewal in the Catholic Church, Newman is seen to have a special ecumenical vocation not only for his own country but also for the whole church. By insisting that 'the Church must be prepared for converts, as well as converts for the Church', he already in a certain measure anticipated in his broad theological vision one of the main aims and orientations of the Second Vatican Council and the Church in the post-Conciliar period. In the spirit of my predecessors in the See of Peter, I express the hope that under this very important aspect, and under other aspects no less important, the figure and teaching of the great Cardinal will continue to inspire an ever more effective fulfilment of the Church's mission in the modern world, and that it will help to renew the spiritual life of her members and hasten the restoration of unity among all Christians."

Archbishop Ramsey of Canterbury was quick to see the significance of Newman's life for the spiritual renewal of both the Catholic and Anglican communities. He wrote: "I am not surprised when I hear it said that the spiritual renewal of the Roman Catholic Church will mean the recapturing of something of the spirit of John Henry Newman. I believe too that the renewal of the Anglican Church will involve the recapturing of something of the spirit of John Henry Newman, and by that I mean not the recapturing of Tractarianism in its particular polemical theses, but rather the recapturing of that spirit of scriptural holiness which pervades his writing from first to last. It was the perception of that which caused Pusey to write only a fortnight after the great grief of 1845, 'As each by God's grace grows in holiness, each Church will recognise more and more the presence of God's Holy Spirit in the other'. The significance for today of John Henry Newman is that he brings this home to us.

This is, I feel, a point of great importance for us also at this time, when a certain amount of impatience and frustration has overtaken our ecumenical endeavours. If we wish to make our contribution to the progress of ecumenism, then we must open our hearts to the movement of the Holy Spirit. To quote the words of Pope Paul VI in St Peter's Basilica, during the visit in 1967 of the Ecumenical Patriarch Athenagoras I to Rome: "Without this effort, which must be unceasing, to be faithful to the Holy Spirit who transforms us into the likeness of his Son, there can be no true lasting brotherhood. It is only by becoming sons in the Son that we also truly become in a mysterious manner brothers of one another."

We are all aware of the intense pain that our divisions cause. There are practical day-to-day problems that urge us on towards a perfect unity in faith, problems such as inter-communion and mixed marriages. Many would like to see easy and immediate solutions to such problems, but we are warned by Newman to be wary of any apparent solution that betrays our whole understanding of Church and Tradition. Newman insisted that the course of Christian unity must necessarily safeguard the truth of revealed doctrine. A clear statement to this effect appears in the *Apologia* (p. 110): "Purity of faith is more precious to the Christian than unity itself." In fact he held doggedly to tenets of doctrine and dogma for the sake of truth, and accepted much suffering and reproach because he preferred the holiness of a clear conscience to the superficial peace of compromise.

But while the whole Christian truth must be spoken without passing over thorny problems in silence or giving way to vague definitions or compromise, Newman makes a point that is vital for progress in all our theological dialogue, namely that doctrine has to be presented in its essential purity, as a whole, without exaggeration or distortion. It is not the theory of this or that theological school that is the object of our dialogue, but the revealed truth itself.

Newman began his spiritual journey untrammelled by a dominant philosophy or tradition of theology. From his evangelical teachers he received the knowledge of the fundamental truths of revelation: the Holy Trinity, the Incarnation, the struggle between good and evil, leading to heaven or to hell. As a young man he added to this basic belief what he learned from his High Church friends concerning the Visible Church, the Sacraments and devotion to the Blessed Virgin Mary. From his study of the bible and of the Fathers of the Church he gradually grew into the whole corpus of Catholic truth, derived from these sources.

Newman had laid it down as "being almost a definition of heresy, that it fastens on some one statement as if it were the whole truth, to the denial of all others, and as a basis of a new faith". But he saw how heresy throws orthodoxy out of its proper proportion and balance, and almost inevitably causes revealed truths, by reaction, to be exaggerated or obscured or distorted. Pope John XXIII was well aware of this problem and at the very beginning of the Second Vatican Council made the distinction that was very clear in Newman's mind, but which in many cases has still to be applied fully in ecumenical dialogue today.

Addressing the Council Fathers on the opening day of the Council, Pope John XXIII explained: "This certain and unchangeable doctrine to which faithful obedience is due, has to be explored and presented in a way that is demanded by our times. The deposit of faith which consists of the truths contained in sacred doctrine, is one thing; the manner of presentation, always however with the same meaning and signification, is always something else."

In Newman we see an integration of heart and mind and will that was unique in its power and in its depth. The witness of his person is a judgment on any superficiality or insincerity in our ecumenical engagements. We must be involved personally as well as intellectually with our partners in other Churches and ecclesial communities. Those with long experience in ecumenical dialogue know how enriching but also how costly this experience can be. It is an experience, however, that must be shared more widely if ecumenism is to find deep roots in the Christian culture of today.

Newman lived long before the days of ecumenical dialogue. But his mind, his sympathies, his affections, his whole attitude to people and to the mystery of God teach us most eloquently about the ecumenical movement and may suggest to each of us in a very personal way, what could be our role within it. May the Holy Spirit heal and restore us, thus making us fit instruments for the fulfillment of the prayer of Christ that "they may all be one." (Jn 17:21).

Letter from Pope John Paul II
to Vincent Nichols, Archbishop of Birmingham

On the occasion of the second centenary of the birth of the Venerable Servant of God John Henry Newman, I gladly join you, your Brother Bishops of England and Wales, the priests of the Birmingham Oratory and a host of voices throughout the world in praising God for the gift of the great English Cardinal and for his enduring witness.

As Newman pondered the mysterious divine plan unfolding in his own life, he came to a deep and abiding sense that "God has created me to do him some definite service. He has committed some work to me which he has not committed to another. I have my mission" *(Meditations and Devotions)*. How true that thought now appears as we consider his long life and the influence which he has had beyond death. He was born at a particular time – 21 February 1801, in a particular place – London; and to a particular family – the firstborn of John Newman and Jemima Fourdrinier. But the particular mission entrusted to him by God ensures that John Henry Newman belongs to every time and place and people.

Newman was born in troubled times which knew not only political and military upheaval but also turbulence of soul. Old certitudes were shaken, and believers were faced with the threat of rationalism on the one hand and fideism on the other. Rationalism brought with it a rejection of both authority and transcendence, while fideism turned from the challenges of history and the tasks of this world to a distorted dependence upon authority and the supernatural. In such a world, Newman came eventually to a remarkable synthesis of faith and reason which were for him "like two wings on which the human spirit rises to the contemplation of the truth" *(Fides et Ratio,* Introduction; cf. *ibid.,* 74). It was the passionate contemplation of truth which also led him to a liberating acceptance of the authority which has its roots in Christ, and to the sense of the supernatural which opens the human mind and heart to the full range of possibilities revealed in Christ. "Lead kindly light amid the encircling gloom, lead Thou me on", Newman wrote in *The Pillar of the Cloud;* and for him Christ was the light at the heart of every kind of darkness. For his tomb he chose the inscription: *Ex umbris et imaginibus in veritatem;* and it was clear at the end of his life's journey that Christ was the truth he had found.

But Newman's search was shot through with pain. Once he had come to that unshakeable sense of the mission entrusted to him by God, he declared: "Therefore, I will trust him ... If I am in sickness, my sickness may serve Him, in perplexity, my perplexity may serve Him ... He does nothing in vain ... He may take away my friends. He may throw me among strangers. He may make me feel desolate, make my spirits sink, hide the future from me. Still, He knows what He is about" *(Meditations and Devotions)*. All these trials he knew in his life; but rather than diminish or destroy him they paradoxically strengthened his faith in the God who had called him, and confirmed him in the conviction that God "does nothing in vain". In the end, therefore, what shines forth in Newman is the mystery of the Lord's Cross: this was the heart of his mission, the absolute truth which he contemplated, the "kindly light" which led him on.

As we thank God for the gift of the Venerable John Henry Newman on the two hundredth anniversary of his birth, we pray that this sure and eloquent guide in our perplexity will also become for us in all our needs a powerful intercessor before the throne of grace. Let us pray that the time will soon come when the Church can officially and publicly proclaim the exemplary holiness of Cardinal John Henry Newman, one of the most distinguished and versatile champions of English spirituality. With my Apostolic Blessing

From the Vatican
22 January 2001
Joannes Paulus II

Cardinal Cormac Murphy-O'Connor, Archbishop of Westminster, pictured in Newman's private chapel at the Oratory House, Birmingham, on 21 February 2002.

Courtesy of the Fathers of the Birmingham Oratory

Close of the Newman Bicentenary Year

21 February 2002

The Cardinal Newman Bicentenary Year was brought to an end on 21 February 2002, with a "Musical Oratory" a service of prayer and preaching, and choral and chamber music at the Oratory Church Birmingham, in the presence of Cardinal Cormac Murphy-O'Connor, Archbishop of Westminster and President of the Bishops' Conference of England and Wales.

Cardinal Cormac Murphy-O'Connor: Opening Address

Father Provost, fellow guests, Bishop Philip, dear friends, it is a great pleasure for me to be with you this evening to mark the close of the Bicentenary Year honouring the Venerable John Henry Cardinal Newman. I don't suppose there is a person in this church who doesn't know who Newman was. Most of us, I suspect, have a very personal interest in him and will have been moved by an encounter, literary or spiritual, or most likely both, with either his obvious holiness, his towering intellect, or his uncompromising devotion to the Church and her development.

Newman was the quintessential man of faith and of reason. The man wedded to truth, mindful not only of the tradition of the Church, but of the vital importance of an informed conscience. A man at once completely of his time – a time of great upheaval in the Church – and, in so many ways, far ahead of his time.

And not without a sense of humour either. Surely there was a twinkle in his eye as well as a hint of steel, when he famously toasted "conscience first, and the Pope afterwards". In truth a man of great joy and great sorrow whose *capax dei* revealed itself in some of the most sublime creative writing in the English language.

Newman knew dark times, the loss of friends, a life among strangers, feelings of desolation, depression and bewilderment; that's a fair description of much of his Catholic life, at least until the *Apologia* and later when he became a Cardinal. And yet I draw inspiration from the fact that in spite of severe trials, he never lost hope. It should be the same for each of us, not only as individuals, but in our service of the Church. Not for nothing I chose the epithet "Joy and Hope, *Gaudium et Spes*" for my motto, both as a bishop and when I followed Newman and was made Cardinal.

John Henry Newman c 1840 by Maria Giberne.
Courtesy of the Fathers of the Birmingham Oratory

Part eight

Newman and Oxford

Pope Paul VI with Fr Stephen Dessain, Archivist at the Birmingham Oratory and Editor, *The Letters and Diaries of John Henry Newman,* at the Apostolic Palace in the Vatican during the Holy Year 1975. A Papal Audience was granted to the participants of the Newman Symposium in April, organised by the International Centre of Newman Friends.

L'Osservatore Romano

Newman and Oxford

Address given by Fr Stephen Dessain at the University Church
of St Mary the Virgin, Oxford, 17 September 1963.

It would be ungracious if I did not begin by expressing what must be in many minds, very great appreciation of the act of Dr Cross, and the Vicar of St Mary's in arranging the commemoration of Newman, which comes so very appropriately during the Patristic Conference.

Newman and Oxford: the two names are inextricably intertwined, but if we are to understand how they reacted upon each other, we must remind ourselves of what Newman was like when, on 8 June 1817, at the age of sixteen-and-a-half, he came into residence in "the sacred city of Anglicanism". What was his religious state when he entered what he was later to describe as: "The most religious university in the world"?[1]

During the autumn of 1816, at Ealing School, he had embraced wholeheartedly the Christian faith, in the purest form available to him. It was a kind of evangelical conversion, but already he was prepared to give a reason for the faith that was in him. From now on the Incarnation and the Blessed Trinity, and the struggle between good and evil, which led ultimately to heaven or hell, were no more mere abstract doctrines. He began to realise and live them. With his mind he accepted the revealed religion of Christianity, and with his heart he embraced its ideal of holiness.

As an undergraduate and Scholar of Trinity his resolution was put to the test. He stood out against customs we associate rather with eighteenth century Oxford. He lived a life of prayer, recollection and hard work. Yet he did not become morose. On the contrary – the friends who were to be found about him in such numbers all his life long, gathered about him already.

But Trinity had no influence on his religious development. In the *Apologia* he passed straight from the account of his first conversion to the consequences of his election to the Oriel Fellowship in 1822. At Trinity there lingered the man of the previous generation, whom Newman has described: "Oxford was his home, and with the advantages of home it had the disadvantages; it was a very dear place, but a very idle one; it was one long vacation."[2] But Newman was later to say that if he: "had to choose between a so-called University which dispensed with residence and tutorial superintendence, and gave its degrees to any person who passed an examination", and one which "merely brought a number of young men together for three of four years", he would prefer the latter as more successful in enlarging the mind and preparing a man for the world.[3] We can understand then Newman's exclamation about Trinity, when describing his departure from Oxford: "Trinity, so dear to me, and which held on its foundation so many who

---

[1] *Essays Critical and Historical* II, p. 408. This and subsequent references are to the uniform edition of Newman's works, published by Longmans.
[2] *Historical Sketches* III, p. 316.
[3] *Idea of a University*, p. 145.

have been kind to me both when I was a boy, and all through my Oxford life. Trinity has never been unkind to me."[4]

Nonetheless, when Newman became a tutor at Oriel he tried to remedy the defects of Oxford education. He considered he held a pastoral office and must try to influence those under him. "I have known a time…", he wrote long afterwards, "when things went for the most part by mere routine, and form took the place of earnestness … in which teachers were cut off from the taught by an insurmountable barrier; when neither party entered into the thoughts of the other … when a tutor was supposed to fulfil his duty if he trotted like a squirrel in his cage, if at a certain hour he was in a certain room … and when neither the one nor the other dreamed of seeing each other out of lecture, out of chapel, or out of academical gown."[5] This was the reign of law without influence, of system without personality. It was not the way of Newman, who chose for his motto as a Cardinal, *Cor ad Cor Loquitur*; but his plans were thwarted by the Provost of Oriel, and after a few years he found himself without pupils.

Looking back we can see that this enforced idleness was providential. It freed Newman for his mission. Nor was it for this negative blessing only that he had cause to be grateful to Oriel. There his mind was trained, and there, thanks to his own industriousness, and also thanks to John Keble and Richard Hurrell Froude, he completed his hold on the revealed truths of Christianity. From them he learned that the Church was a visible institution reaching back to our Lord Jesus Christ, and that the sacraments were his instruments for working upon us. Hurrell Froude in particular fixed deep in Newman "the idea of devotion to the Blessed Virgin" and led him "gradually to believe in the Real Presence."[6]

From childhood he had imbibed Holy Scripture and now he studied systematically that other source of revealed religion, the Fathers of the Church. These he had fallen in love with as soon as he encountered them in Milner's *Church History*, which he read at the time of his first conversion. From 1828 onwards he began to read them scientifically. There is no need in such a gathering as this to explain what Newman found in this authentic source – and one so neglected at that time. He collected a splendid patristic library, which followed him eventually to Littlemore and Birmingham, and there is ample evidence in his writings, published and unpublished, to show how thoroughly he studied the Fathers.

For how much then he had to be grateful to Oxford and Oriel: "Had I not come to Oxford", he exclaimed in the *Apologia*, "perhaps I never should have heard of the visible Church, or of Tradition or other Catholic doctrines".[7] And a few years earlier in 1860 he wrote: "Catholics did not make us Catholics, Oxford made us Catholics."[8]

We may say that at the end of his first decade at Oriel Newman had grasped almost the whole cycle of revealed truth. "I held a large bold system of religion very unlike the

---

[4] *Apologia pro vita sua*, p. 237.
[5] *Historical Sketches* III, pp. 75-6.
[6] *Apologia*, p. 25.
[7] *Apologia*, p. 341.
[8] Letter of 2 June 1860, to E E Estcourt (*Letters and Diaries of John Henry Newman* (ed. Charles Stephen Dessain) (London, 1969)) XIX, pp. 351-53.

Protestantism of the day",[9] while on the other hand in England around him "the very notion of the Church Catholic had died away from men's minds."[10]

Newman's devotion to Revealed Religion gives his life an extraordinary unity. He embraced it with all his heart just before coming to Oxford; there he lived it and completed his knowledge of it – now he was to come forward as its much needed champion. "I had a supreme confidence in our cause; we were upholding that primitive Christianity which was delivered for all time by the early teachers of the Church, and which was registered and attested in the Anglican formularies and by the Anglican divines. That ancient religion had well-nigh faded out of the land."[11]

Nine years of success lay before Newman, who was described at this time as looking like Julius Caesar – years of intense activity, writing, preaching, organising, and every meal-time utilised for meetings with friends or helpers or others, perhaps to be won over. His extraordinary ascendancy was the fruit of his prayerfulness and detachment. That judge of men, the old President of Magdalen, remarked of Newman, different from so many of his contemporaries: "I am sure he is not looking to get on in life."[12]

The tribute in *The Guardian* at his death, probably by Dean Church, has described the debt of Anglicanism to him. He was: "The founder of the Church of England as we see it. What the Church of England would have become without the Tractarian Movement we can faintly guess, and of the Tractarian Movement Newman was the living soul and the inspiring genius."[13]

Newman's sermons in this church represent the Oxford Movement at its highest. There are many testimonies to their influence on his hearers, but they were even more influential as they spread in print through the English-speaking world. Revealed truth was made real, and many first began to lead a spiritual life after reading them. To quote Dean Church once more: "The most practical of sermons ... they are also intensely dogmatic" – in Newman dogmas were not hard, but "instinct with truth and life." Dean Church gives two reasons for the effect produced by the sermons: "One was the intense hold which the vast realities of religion had gained on the writer's mind, ... the other was the strong instructive shrinking from anything like personal display." And he sums up Newman's attitude in the Sermons: "If you have a religion like Christianity, think of it and have it worthily."[14]

Besides their importance for the renewal of Anglicanism, Newman's *Parochial Sermons* and the corpus of his Anglican writings have a further great interest and value. The late Abbot Vonier used to sigh for a classical theology, where every truth of revelation would be stated in its proper proportion and balance, and not, as is so often inevitable, distorted or exaggerated or obscured by reaction against heresy.[15] Of course it is impossible for anyone to work out the doctrines of Christianity from their various sources, completely *in vacuo*.

[9] *Apologia*, p. 93.
[10] *Essays Critical and Historical* II, pp. 408–9.
[11] *Apologia*, p. 43.
[12] Middleton, *Newman at Oxford* (London, 1950), p. 121.
[13] *The Guardian*, 13 August 1890.
[14] *Occasional Papers* II (London, 1897), pp. 457–9, 449–51.
[15] Anscar Vonier, *The New and Eternal Covenant*, London, 1930, pp. 1–11.

But Newman was in a strikingly privileged position. Unlike the Roman theologians, he was brought up under the influence of no dominant philosophy or tradition of theology. If he made use of the Anglican divines, it was, as he confessed, rather to protect and defend what he had already elaborated from Holy Scripture and the Fathers. If he reacted against heresy, it was against the general heresy which rejected all revealed religion. And so it comes about that in his Anglican writings we can find a classical, a truly catholic Catholicism.

One example of this is his treatment in *Lectures on Justification* of the doctrine of grace, which he lifted above the controversies, and brought back to the essential Gift of God himself, the Presence of the Father, the Son and the Holy Spirit in every true Christian. Another significant example is his teaching on the Church, about which as an Evangelical he had no adequate conception. He might so easily have run to the other extreme, and, as was common in his day, have identified the Church with its Hierarchy. No, the Church was the community of the faithful, of all those who had received the Holy Spirit. Thus not only the bishops but the Christian people possessed the faith, they preserved it, and they were to be consulted to discover it. It is no wonder, when the Church of Rome calls a Council in order to present herself and her teaching before the world in their primitive attractiveness and splendour, that her theologians should increasingly draw inspiration from Newman. Thus again and again one is told that the Second Vatican Council is "Newman's Council."

And from this we are led to another conclusion – how valuable Newman is for the further, more distant ecumenical aim of the Council. His exposition of the Christian faith is a bridge. Or, as Fr Thomas Satory wrote recently: "Both Anglicans and Catholics possess an exponent of the ecumenical spirit *par excellence* in John Henry Newman … Newman is of such special importance to us because he represents a Catholicism that is truly catholic, that is to say all embracing, and thus integrates legitimate concerns of the reformers into Catholicism."[16]

But we must return to Newman and Oxford. The Tractarian Movement by its very nature was a movement for the unity of Christians. At the beginning of it Newman had written: "Considering the high gifts and the strong claims of the Church of Rome and her dependencies on our admiration, reverence, love and gratitude, how could we withstand her as we do; how could we refrain from being melted into tenderness, and rushing into communion with her, but for the words of Truth, which bid us prefer itself to the whole world?"[17] When his hesitations began in 1839 he drew up prayers for unity; and when he left the Church of England, it was because he considered that the claims of unity and the teachings of Revealed Religion made it his duty to do so.

The wrench was a terrible one and Newman imposed on himself the further wrench of leaving Oxford because he would not act in direct hostility to the Church of England. In 1860 he wrote: "While I do not see my way to weaken the Church of England, being what it is, least of all should I be disposed to do so in Oxford, which has hitherto been the seat of those traditions which constitute whatever there is of Catholic doctrine and

---

[16] Thomas Satory OSB, *The Oecumenical Movement and the Unity of the Church*, Oxford, 1963, p. vi.

[17] Records of the Church VI, quoted in the preface to *The Development of Christian Doctrine.*

practice in the Anglican Church. Oxford deserves least of any part of Anglican territory to be interfered with. That there are false traditions there I know well … but till things are very much changed there, in weakening Oxford, we are weakening our friends, weakening our own *de facto paidagogos* into the Church … I should have the greatest repugnance to introducing controversy into these quiet circles and sober schools of thought, which are the strength of the Church of England … In all that I have written, I have spoken of Oxford and the Oxford system with affection and admiration. I have put its system forward as an instance of that union of dogmatic teaching and liberal education which command my assent."[18]

When a few years later there was a question of a return of Newman himself to Oxford, he wrote to reassure Pusey: "I should come to Oxford for the sake of the Catholic youth there, who are likely to be, in the future, more numerous than they are now, and my first object after that would be to soften prejudice against Catholicism. Personally, it would be as painful a step as I could be called to make."[19]

Newman hoped to bring his Oratory of St Philip to Oxford, his Oratory which relied on influence rather than discipline, and which was a continuation of his community at Littlemore, just as Littlemore was in some sense an effort to fulfil what had been prevented at Oriel. Newman was prepared to do what was personally so painful in order to enable the minority group he had joined to profit by what Oxford had to give. To those of us, members of this group, who have been at Oxford since his day, the reasons put forward to forbid his return appear without foundation and even ludicrous.

There are many testimonies to Newman's enduring love for Oxford, long before his visit in 1878, when Trinity made him the first of her honorary fellows. John Pollen, when he met him in Dublin in 1855, described him as: "quite charming, so very simple and so fond of his old Oxford recollections".[20] To Isaac Williams, Newman wrote in 1863: "Of all human things, perhaps Oxford is dearest to my heart, and some parsonages in the country".

Yet he knew it could no longer be called: "the most religious university in the world." In the *Letter to the Duke of Norfolk* he said: "No one mourns … more than I over the state of Oxford, given up, alas!, to 'Liberalism and Progress', to the forfeiture of her great medieval motto *'Dominus Illuminatio mea'*."[21] He knew that at Oxford as elsewhere the struggle for Revealed Religion was in many ways a losing one. Yet for this struggle also, during the Tractarian Movement, he had provided in his *Sermons Preached before the University of Oxford*, a reasonable basis and defence of the Christian faith, appreciated at the time, perhaps even more appreciated now. Of rationalism Pusey remarked that "Newman while he was with us was its most powerful and successful antagonist."[22] He managed to show also how liberalism and progress had their place in a truly Catholic scheme.

Perhaps it may be permissible to conclude with one more quotation from Newman. It was an appeal made to Oxford, in 1838, when his position in the Movement was at its

[18] Letters of 2 and 10 June 1860 to E.E. Estcourt; *Letters and Diaries* XIX, pp. 351-53, 359-60.

[19] Letter of 29 April 1866 to E. B. Pusey; *Letters and Diaries* XXII, p. 227.

[20] Anne Pollen, *John Hungerford Pollen,* London, 1920, p. 253.

[21] *Difficulties of Anglicans* II, p. 268.

[22] H P Liddon, *Life of Edward Bouverie Pusey* III, London, 1893, p.116.

height, and before the least doubt had touched him: "It really is losing time and toil to deny, what is as plain as day, that Oxford has, and ever has had, what men of the world will call a Popish character, that in opinion and tone of thought its members are the successors of the old monks, or that those who now speak against Wesleyans and Independents, would also have opposed the Foxes and Knoxes of the Reformation. Surely it is our wisdom, as we follow, so to profess to follow ancient times. Let us not fear to connect ourselves with our predecessors; let us discern in our beautiful homes the awful traces of the past, and the past will stand by us. Let us stand upon the vestiges of the old city, and with the hero in the poet's romance, we shall find a talisman amid the ruins. 'The talisman is faith'."[23]

The College, Littlemore, where John Henry Newman was received into the Catholic Church on 9 October 1845.

Courtesy of the Fathers of the Birmingham Oratory

In June 1986, the Fathers of the Birmingham Oratory, who own The College, invited the Sisters of The Work to come to Littlemore, to undertake its day-to-day care and to welcome pilgrims. Newman's own oratory in The College is now a prayerful chapel and the Sisters have also created a Newman Library and a permanent exhibition. These facilities mean that The College has become a centre for prayer and study for pilgrims and scholars from around the world. Since 1987 the guest-books show that Littlemore has welcomed more than 35,000 visitors.

---

[23] *Historical Sketches* III, p.333.

John Henry Newman by George Richmond, 1844.

Courtesy of the Fathers of the Birmingham Oratory

Dr Newman preaching at the University Church of St Mary the Virgin, Oxford in 1841. Sketch published by Ryan, High Street, Oxford.

Courtesy of the Fathers of the Birmingham Oratory

Centenary of the Election of
John Henry Newman as Honorary Fellow
of Trinity College, Oxford

Sermon by the Rev Dr Geoffrey Rowell,
Chaplain, Keble College, Oxford, 11 June 1977

"He was a good man, and full of the Holy Ghost and of faith" (Acts 11:24) It was this text which John Henry Newman took for the sermon on the Feast of St Barnabas which is printed in the second volume of his *Parochial and Plain Sermons.* On this feast of St Barnabas, when we commemorate the centenary of Newman's election as an Honorary Fellow of Trinity, his old college, and as the first Honorary Fellow that the College had elected, it is by no means inappropriate to take those words from Acts as indicating the pattern of Christian holiness which John Henry Newnan strove to embody in his life.

Speaking on sanctity in that sermon on St Barnabas, Newman reminded his hearers that the divine grace by which men are brought to sanctity does not destroy nature but fulfils it, and that the saints of God are not those whose individuality has been crushed. "The especial grace poured upon the Apostles and their associates, whether miraculous or moral, had no tendency to destroy their respective peculiarities of temper and character, to invest them with a sanctity beyond our imitation, or to preclude failings and errors which may be our warning. It left them, as it found them, men."

And Newman went on to say in this sermon that the saints are not those who exhibit a total perfection, but are rather those in whom we see particular graces exemplified, and in whom we see also other facets of character which serve as warnings rather than as examples – and he cites the "immature ardour" of James and John, the "sudden fall" of Peter, and the "cowardice" of Mark, and what he sees as Barnabas' lack of "firmness, manliness, and godly severity" in his joining Peter in yielding to the demands of the Judaizers who would not eat with Gentiles. The perfection of the saints of God is reserved for heaven, what we see here is the work of God's grace in the lives of those who live by faith.

It is sanctity of that kind that I believe we can discern in the life of John Henry Newman. In the particular circumstances of his day he endeavoured to live, and to encourage others to live. by a sure and certain faith in the reality of God, and of a God who had given himself into the world in Christ "for us men and for our salvation."

Newman was aware of the perennial temptation to turn Christianity into a concept, to make a faith which was life and power disclosed in particular deeds and acts into the abstractions and speculation of a religion of notions. Himself endowed with brilliant intellectual gifts, he was aware that the Christian faith, if it were true, must be true for those without such abilities, and that in whatever way the reasonableness of belief might be shown to those who found faith a stumbling-block, that way could never be a way which had the effect of making Christianity into the preserve of academics. Newman did not try to set down a theory of how men ought to believe, he sought to explore how men actually did believe, how that faith was related to human understanding and reason, and how it was expressed in life. In one of his Sermons on Subjects of the Day he seeks to reassure those who feel themselves threatened by the accusations that they have only a hereditary religion, that they might believe what they believe, and practise what they practise, "because they have been taught so to do, without any reasons of their own."

Newman admits that such people may not be able to produce reasons, that they have never analyzed their convictions, but that is not the same as saying that they do not have reasons. "It does not", says Newman, "make a man more religious that he knows why and how he became so." Our religious faith may, indeed usually does, begin by being hereditary, "yet for all that, it may be much more than hereditary, when we have lived long enough to have made trial of it, and that, although we have not the skill to bring out into words the details and the results of that trial, or to show in a clear logical form that we have this or that good reason for believing." Furthermore, many who are the most skilled religious controversialists, may be properly accused of being adherents of a merely hereditary religion, but hereditary in the sense of its being gleaned second-hand from the arguments of controversial divinity.

And so, Newman goes on: "He who has the truth within him, though he cannot evolve it out of his heart in shape or proportions for another's inspection, is blessed beyond all comparison above him, who has much to say, and says what is true, but says it not from himself but by rote, and could say quite as well just the reverse, did it so happen that he mistook it for truth ... Surely, as the only true religion is that which is seated within us, a matter, not of words, but of things, so the only satisfactory test of religion is something within us. If religion be a personal matter, its reasons should also be personal. Wherever it is present, in the world or in the heart, it produces an effect, and that effect is its evidence ... This is the secret reason why religious men believe, whether they are adequately conscious of it or not; whether they can put it into words or no; their past experience that the doctrine which they hold is a reality in their minds, not a mere opinion, and has come to them, "not in word, but in power ..." A man's real reason for attachment to his own religious communion ... is not any series of historical or philosophical arguments, not any thing merely beautiful in its system ... but what it has done for him and others; his confidence in it as a means by which men be brought nearer to God, and may become better and happier."

It was in 1816, the year to which he was entered at Trinity ("A most gentleman-like College" as his Ealing Headmaster described it) that the Christian faith became for Newman a reality and power. It was "an inward conversion" of which, at the time of writing the *Apologia* so many years later, he said that he was still more certain than that he had hands and feet. The experience of the reality of God which Newman had at this time remained with him, giving an inner consistency to his life. As he puts it in an early note: "The unconverted man changes his end with his time of life, or goes on changing about – but here it is all reality."

Newman would speak much of change – "here below to live is to change, and to be perfect is to have changed often"; his sense of history was such that he was well aware of the change and development of doctrinal expression, and gave us one of the most theologically perceptive accounts of that development at a time when many Christian thinkers held a static view of scriptural texts and doctrinal definitions torn out of their historical contexts.

Change there was for Newman but it was not a change of the end towards which his life was directed: that remained constant. The young Newman who prayed, when on the advice of his tutor he had put in for a Trinity scholarship, that God would preserve him from relying too much on getting the scholarship and would keep him from glorying in his success if he gained it, is continuous with the Catholic Newman praying to God: "If thou givest me health and strength and success in this world, keep me ever on my guard lest these great gifts carry me away from thee." The words echo the earlier prayer: "Let me not be lead away from thee by the hopes of it. May I so dispose myself that I may praise thy name, whether I receive what I pray for, or whether I receive it not."

His sensitivity to others, their feelings and prejudices and convictions, was likewise continuous. At the time when he was preparing to visit Oxford in 1878 to dine here at Trinity to mark his election as an Honorary Fellow, he wished to dedicate a new edition of the *Essay on Development*. He wished to dedicate this to President Wayte, but feared that it might be offensive.

Newman was concerned lest it might be thought that he was beginning a crusade, or lest Trinity might think he was trying to twist their generosity in making him an honorary Fellow into a point of denominational advantage. His friend, Dean Church, assured him this was not the case. This same sensitivity, which at times made Newman seem 'prickly' to those with whom he had to deal, also made him skilled in the art of communication by entering into the situation and outlook of others and leading them on to share more nearly his own understanding and outlook. We can catch a hint of it, I believe, in the editorial, which Newman wrote for the short-lived journal *The Undergraduate,* that he and his friend Bowden published during their time at Trinity.

Speaking of the essayist, Newman writes: "It is his greatest art to insinuate himself into the affections of his readers, by accommodating himself to their dispositions, conforming himself to their tastes and studying their pursuits: he must disperse the cloud of prejudice, rather by the soft influence of the sun, than by the violence of the blast; and obtain admirers by adaptation to the times, rather than by novelty of execution." There is an anticipation here of that sense of reserve, combined with the idea of an 'economy' or 'dispensation', which Newman saw as the way of the Church's preaching and teaching, and a way that was grounded in the pattern of God's own communication of himself to man.

To speak of reserve reminds us immediately of the sense of reverence and awe and wonder, which Newman, along with Keble and Pusey and the other leaders of the Oxford Movement, strove to restore to the Church of England. God was holy – he was not to be spoken of as a theory or an abstraction; God was holy – theology must be rooted in prayer and worship, and that prayer and worship must lead men to an awareness of the transcendent mystery of their Lord and Creator, who yet drew near to them in word and in sacrament. Newman's Trinity tutor, Thomas Short, was described as "a high and dry Tory churchman, who would see nothing specially incongruous in a bishop discussing the breed of sheep through the broken window of a church during the pauses in a confirmation service," and who would speak of himself as going to St Nicholas, Abingdon to give "hay and turnips" (i.e. prayers plus sermon) in the morning, and "hay only" (prayers alone) in the afternoon. The high view of the church which the Oxford Movement was concerned to renew was very different. It was sacramental, both in its stress on the centrality of the Eucharist, and in its understanding of the created order as that which was good and to be used in all its richness in worship, and in its awareness of the church as a divine society.

For Newman in particular this understanding of the church was grounded in his patristic knowledge, and in his writing and preaching he sought to express this for the men of his own day. And if Newman today is of special ecumenical significance in the growing together of Anglicans and Roman Catholics, it is not only because being formed in the Church of England, he took that spiritual formation with him to blossom and flourish in the communion of the See of Rome – though that is of great importance; it is because his patristically grounded theology reaches back behind the many divisions of the sixteenth century, and so anticipates in a measure the way of reconciliation of the recent agreed statements. In a way also we can see Trinity's election of Newman to an Honorary Fellowship as the next sign of reconciliation between Anglicans and Roman Catholics who had been so bitterly divided. Newman could have wished no more attractive compliment. As he wrote to one of his friends at the time:

> My dear old first College, Trinity, has made me an honorary Fellow of
> their Society. My affections have ever been with my first College, though
> I have more and more intimately personal Oriel friends. There was too
> much painful at Oriel to allow of its remberance being sweet and dear;
> hence I rejoice that it is Trinity, not Oriel, that has reclaimed me.

And as here in Trinity chapel, where Newman made his first communion, we give thanks for his life and teaching, may we not together claim him as a sign of that unity for which the Lord himself prayed, and of that holiness to which all of us are called and without which we cannot see God?

Mass to commemorate

John Henry Cardinal Newman

Trinity College Chapel, Oxford, 13 May 2005

Cardinal Jean-Marie Lustiger presided and preached at Mass in Trinity College, Oxford, on 13 May 2005, to commemorate the life of Cardinal Newman, one of Trinity's most notable alumni, as part of the College's 450th anniversary celebrations.

At the start of Mass, held in the College chapel, the retired Archbishop of Paris read a letter from Pope Benedict XVI to mark the historic occasion. During the Offertory the evocative words and melody of Newman's great hymn *Lead, kindly light,* written while he was becalmed in a boat off Sicily in 1833, filled the old chapel, as the rays of the mid-May afternoon sunshine shone through the stained-glass windows.

Among the concelebrants at the Mass, on the Feast of Our Lady of Fatima, was Fr Paul Chavasse, Provost of the Birmingham Oratory, and Postulator of the Cause for the beatification and canonization of the Venerable John Henry Cardinal Newman.

The President of Trinity College, Michael Beloff QC, welcomed Cardinal Lustiger at the start of Mass:

> Cardinal Newman is laid claim to by many educational institutions, and indeed had links with other Oxford colleges, but Trinity was his first and deepest love as his undergraduate letters to his mother vividly illustrate. Newman felt deeply honoured by Trinity's invitation to become the College's first ever Honorary Fellow in 1877. It was a symbolic gesture of the reconciliation between England's Catholics and Oxford's Anglican establishment which he himself had done so much to effect.

The Chaplain Fellow, Canon Trevor Williams, added a few words about the significance of Trinity Chapel:

> The college was founded in 1555, exactly 450 years ago, by Sir Thomas Pope, who had been treasurer of the court of Augmentations under Henry VIII. Sir Thomas later served as a leading Privy Counsellor of Queen Mary. However, there had been a college on this site long before that, Durham College, founded in 1286. It was one of the dependent cells of the great Benedictine Abbey of St Cuthbert and was established to provide an education for the monks of Durham. But when the monasteries were suppressed by Henry VIII, Durham College suffered a similar fate.
>
> After a few years the site was acquired by Sir Thomas Pope, and during the reign of Philip and Mary he founded the College dedicated to the One Holy and undivided Trinity. The Chapel was central to the

life of the young college. Mass was celebrated daily, and all the fellows were expected to proceed to the priesthood.

The old Durham College Chapel had become, 'infirm and ruinous' by the time of the Restoration. The new chapel, where we are now, was built and consecrated in 1694, and has remained almost unchanged except for the 19th century stained glass windows. Most of these very fittingly depict saints associated with Durham, with St Cuthbert and St Benedict portrayed opposite me. The chapel was very important to Newman; it's where he took his first communion, and he kept a photo of the interior in his rooms at the Oratory.

The Chapel remains a place where all members of the College are welcome to attend services, or simply to come for quiet meditation and prayer. For many years Catholic mass has been celebrated here once a term, but this is a very special occasion to honour a very special old member, John Henry Newman, who contributed much to the Anglican as well as to the Roman Catholic churches. We can all give thanks to God for his life and work.

Cardinal Jean-Marie Lustiger, Archbishop Emeritus of Paris, with the Honourable Michael Beloff QC, President of Trinity College, Oxford, and Fr Paul Chavasse, Postulator of the Newman Cause, photographed beside the Broadbent bust of Cardinal Newman in the College grounds, after Mass on 13 May 2005.

Photograph by Peter Jennings

Letter from Benedict XVI
to Cardinal Jean-Marie Lustiger
Archbishop Emeritus of Paris

I was pleased to learn that you have been invited to offer Holy Mass at Trinity College, Oxford, as part of the celebrations marking the 450th anniversary of the establishment of that distinguished institution, which was the beloved alma mater of John Henry Cardinal Newman and which later elected him its first Honorary Fellow.

It was at Trinity College that the young Newman learned those habits of mind and heart which guided him through a life of disciplined commitment to the pursuit of religious truth. May his example continue to inspire new generations of students to draw abundantly from the richness of the Christian tradition in order to respond to the deepest yearnings of the human spirit and to draw men and women in every age to Jesus Christ, "the Way, and the Truth and the Life" (Jn 14:6) in the communion of his Mystical Body, the Church.

With these sentiments, I ask you kindly to convey my prayerful good wishes for the anniversary celebrations. Upon all taking part, and in particular the members of the College and their families, I cordially invoke God's blessings of joy and peace.

From the Vatican,
11 May 2005
Signed Benedictus PP XVI

A large screen in St Peter's Square shows the Cardinal Electors inside the Sistine Chapel, at the start of the Conclave on the afternoon of Monday 18 April 2005. The small temporary chimney, from which white smoke indicates the election of the new Bishop of Rome, is visible on the roof of the chapel.

Photograph by Peter Jennings

Part nine

Benedict XVI

Election

First Blessing

First Homily

Inaugural Mass

Pope Benedict XVI appeared on the central loggia of St Peter's Basilica, shortly after his election as Bishop of Rome and Successor of St Peter on 19 April 2005.

Fotografia Felici

Habemus Papam
Cardinal Joseph Ratzinger
19 April 2005

Cardinal Joseph Ratzinger, Dean of the College of Cardinals, was elected the Successor of Saint Peter, and Pontiff of the Roman Catholic Church, during the fourth ballot held in the Sistine Chapel on Tuesday, 19 April 2005. He chose the name Benedict XVI.

At 5.50 pm white smoke, indicating that the Cardinals had elected a Pope, rose from the little temporary chimney on the roof of the Sistine Chapel. Shortly afterwards the great bells of St Peter's Basilica began to ring out as people ran from every direction into the Square. The atmosphere was electric and the anticipation enormous.

At 6.43 pm Cardinal Jorge Medina Estevez appeared on the central loggia of St Peter's Basilica. The huge crowd fell silent as the Chilean cardinal began to speak in Latin.

> *"Annuntio vobis gaudium magnum.*
> *Habemus Papam,"* the cardinal proclaimed.
> *"Eminentissimum ac Reverendissimum Dominum,*
> *Dominum Josephum."* (There were gasps from the crowd).
> *"Sanctae Romanae Ecclesiae Cardinalem Ratzinger*
> *Qui sibi nomen imposuit Benedictum XVI."*

> "I announce to you with great joy;
> We have a Pope;
> The most eminent and most reverend Lord,
> Lord Joseph
> Cardinal of the Holy Roman Church Ratzinger
> Who has taken the name Benedict XVI."

Pope Benedict XVI greets the huge crowd in St Peter's Square from the central loggia of St Peter's Basilica, shortly after his election on 19 April 2005.

Fotografia Felici

First message and blessing of Benedict XVI

St Peter's Square, 19 April 2005

"A simple and humble labourer,
in the vineyard of the Lord"

At 6.48 pm, a smiling Benedict XVI, preceded by the Cross appeared through the parted red curtains. He waved to the thousands of people who packed St Peter's Square and the surrounding streets. The crowds clapped and cheered in joyful celebration. The cardinals who crowded into the loggias either side, looked pleased with a job well done. Before he imparted the traditional Apostolic Blessing, *Urbi et Orbi*, Pope Benedict said a few words in Italian:

Dear Brothers and Sisters,

After the great Pope John Paul II, the Cardinals have elected me, a simple and humble labourer in the vineyard of the Lord.

The fact that the Lord knows how to work and to act, even with inadequate instruments, comforts me, and above all I entrust myself to your prayers.

Let us move forward in the joy of the Risen Lord, confident of his unfailing help. The Lord will help us, and Mary, His Most Holy Mother, will be on our side. Thank you.

At 10.00 am the previous day, Monday 18 April 2005, Cardinal Joseph Ratzinger, Prefect of the Congregation for the Doctrine of the Faith from 1981 until the death of Pope John Paul II on Saturday, 2 April, presided at the Mass *pro eligendo Summo Pontifice,* (for the election of the Supreme Pontiff) concelebrated by all 115 Cardinal Electors in St Peter's Basilica. He delivered a thought-provoking homily, "Let us Ask God for a Pastor to Lead us to Christ".

At 4:30 pm the 115 Cardinal Electors from 52 countries across five continents gathered in the Hall of Blessings. Preceded by the Cross and followed by the Book of Gospels, the Cardinals processed slowly to the nearby Sistine Chapel as the Litany of Saints was sung.

The ceremonies were vividly captured by Vatican Television and transmitted live to a worldwide audience. The historic broadcasts included dramatic scenes from inside the Sistine Chapel, where under the penetrating eye of Michelangelo's *Last Judgement,* the Cardinal Electors placed their right hand on the Book of the Gospels one by one and said aloud the words of the solemn oath. After the singing of the ancient hymn, *Veni, Creator Spiritus*, they pronounced their oath as established by the *Ordo Rituum Conclavis*. The Papal Master of Ceremonies, Archbishop Piero Marini declared *"Extra Omnes!"* ("Everyone Out!").

It was on 16 October 1978 that the College of Cardinals had elected Cardinal Karol Wojtyla, Archbishop of Cracow, the first non-Italian Pope since the sixteenth century, who chose the name Pope John Paul II. Only two of the cardinals who took part in the two Conclaves held during 1978 were present – Cardinal Joseph Ratzinger, and the American, Cardinal William Baum.

The first black smoke rose from the Sistine Chapel chimney at 8.04 pm on Monday 18 April. The following day, Tuesday 19 April, there was black smoke at 11.52 am.

On Saturday, 16 April 2005, the twelfth and last General Congregation of the Sede Vacante (Vacant See) was held in the Vatican. Afterwards, the Director of the Holy See Press Office, Dr Joaquin Navarro-Valls, informed journalists that the Cardinal Camerlengo, Cardinal Eduardo Martinez Somalo, had presented, in everyone's name, best wishes to Cardinal Joseph Ratzinger, Dean of the College of Cardinals, on the occasion of his 78th birthday.

Pope John XXIII, Cardinal Angelo Roncalli, Patriarch of Venice, was 77 years old when he was elected Pope on 28 October 1958. He was described by the media at the time as a 'caretaker' who was unlikely to do much during his Pontificate. He took everyone by surprise and initiated the Second Vatican Council, 1963-1965.

As with Blessed John XXIII, the Papacy of Benedict XVI, under the guidance of the Holy Spirit, will also be full of surprises!

A special miniature sheet of postage stamps issued by Isle of Man Post depicting
John Paul II and Benedict XVI, marking World Youth Day, August 2005.

Communion and Collegiality

First Homily of Benedict XVI

Sistine Chapel, 20 April 2005

Pope Benedict XVI celebrated Mass with members of the College of Cardinals in the Sistine Chapel on the morning of Wednesday 20 April 2005, following his election the previous afternoon. At the end of Mass the new Pope delivered his first homily, in Latin.

Grace and peace in abundance to all of you. In my soul there are two contrasting sentiments in these hours. On the one hand, a sense of inadequacy and human turmoil for the responsibility entrusted to me yesterday as the Successor of the Apostle Peter in this See of Rome, with regard to the Universal Church. On the other hand, I sense within me profound gratitude to God, Who – as the liturgy makes us sing – does not abandon His flock, but leads it throughout time, under the guidance of those whom He has chosen as vicars of His Son, and made pastors.

Dear Ones, this intimate recognition for a gift of divine mercy prevails in my heart in spite of everything. I consider this a grace obtained for me by my venerated predecessor, John Paul II. It seems I can feel his strong hand squeezing mine; I seem to see his smiling eyes and listen to his words, addressed to me especially at this moment: "Do not be afraid!"

The death of the Holy Father John Paul II, and the days which followed, were for the Church and for the entire world an extraordinary time of grace. The great pain for his death and the void that it left in all of us were tempered by the action of the Risen Christ, which showed itself during long days in the choral wave of faith, love and spiritual solidarity, culminating in his solemn funeral.

We can say it: the funeral of John Paul II was a truly extraordinary experience in which was perceived in some way the power of God, Who, through His Church, wishes to form a great family of all peoples, through the unifying force of Truth and Love. In the hour of death, conformed to his Master and Lord, John Paul II crowned his long and fruitful pontificate, confirming the Christian people in faith, gathering them around him and making the entire human family feel more united.

How can one not feel sustained by this witness? How can one not feel the encouragement that comes from this event of grace?

Surprising every prevision I had, Divine Providence through the will of the venerable Cardinal Fathers called me to succeed this great Pope. I have been thinking in these hours about what happened in the region of Cesarea of Phillippi two thousand years ago: I seem to hear the words of Peter: "You are Christ, the Son of the living God," and the solemn affirmation of the Lord: "You are Peter and on this rock I will build my Church ... I will give you the keys of the kingdom of heaven."

You are Christ! You are Peter! It seems I am reliving this very Gospel scene; I, the Successor of Peter, repeat with trepidation the anxious words of the fisherman from Galilee and I listen again with intimate emotion to the reassuring promise of the divine Master. If the weight of the responsibility that now lies on my poor shoulders is enormous, the divine power on which I can count is surely immeasurable: "You are Peter and on this rock I will build my Church". Electing me as the Bishop of Rome, the Lord wanted me as his Vicar, he wished me to be the "rock" upon which everyone may rest with confidence. I ask him to make up for the poverty of my strength, that I may be a courageous and faithful pastor of His flock, always docile to the inspirations of His Spirit.

I undertake this special ministry, the "Petrine" ministry at the service of the Universal Church, with humble abandonment into the hands of the Providence of God. And it is to Christ in the first place that I renew my total and trustworthy adhesion: "*In Te, Domine, speravi; non confundar in aeternum!*"

To you, Lord Cardinals, with a grateful soul for the trust shown me, I ask you to sustain me with prayer and with constant, active and wise collaboration. I also ask my brothers in the episcopacy to be close to me in prayer and counsel so that I may truly be the "*Servus servorum Dei*" ('Servant of the servants of God'). As Peter and the other Apostles were, through the will of the Lord, one apostolic college, in the same way the Successor of Peter and the Bishops, successors of the Apostles – and the Council forcefully repeated this – must be closely united among themselves. This collegial communion, even in the diversity of roles and functions of the Supreme Pontiff and the bishops, is at the service of the Church and the unity of faith from which depend in a notable measure the effectiveness of the evangelizing mission to the contemporary world. This path, upon which my venerated predecessors went forward, I too intend to follow, concerned solely with proclaiming to the world the living presence of Christ.

Before my eyes is, in particular, the witness of Pope John Paul II. He leaves us a Church that is more courageous, freer, younger. A Church that, according to his teaching and example, looks with serenity to the past and is not afraid of the future. With the Great Jubilee the Church was introduced into the new millennium carrying in her hands the Gospel, applied to the world through the authoritative re-reading of Vatican Council II. Pope John Paul II justly indicated the Council as a "compass" with which to orient ourselves in the vast ocean of the third millennium. Also in his spiritual testament he noted: "I am convinced that for a very long time the new generations will draw upon the riches that this council of the 20th century gave us."

I too, as I start in the service that is proper to the Successor of Peter, wish to affirm with force my decided will to pursue the commitment to enact Vatican Council II, in the wake of my predecessors and in faithful continuity with the millennia-old tradition of the Church. Precisely this year is the 40th anniversary of the conclusion of this conciliar assembly (8 December 1965). With the passing of time, the conciliar documents have not lost their timeliness; their teachings have shown themselves to be especially pertinent to the new exigencies of the Church and the present globalized society.

In a very significant way, my pontificate starts as the Church is living the special year dedicated to the Eucharist. How can I not see in this providential coincidence an element that must mark the ministry to which I have been called? The Eucharist, the heart of

Christian life and the source of the evangelizing mission of the Church, cannot but be the permanent centre and the source of the Petrine service entrusted to me.

The Eucharist makes the Risen Christ constantly present, Christ who continues to give himself to us, calling us to participate in the banquet of His Body and His Blood. From this full communion with Him comes every other element of the life of the Church: in the first place the communion among the faithful, the commitment to proclaim and give witness to the Gospel, the ardor of charity towards all, especially towards the poor and the smallest.

In this year, therefore, the Solemnity of Corpus Christi must be celebrated in a particularly special way. The Eucharist will be at the centre, in August, of World Youth Day in Cologne and, in October, of the Ordinary Assembly of the Synod of Bishops which will take place on the theme "*The Eucharist, Source and Summit of the Life and Mission of the Church.*" (2-23 October 2005). I ask everyone to intensify in the coming months love and devotion to the Eucharistic Jesus and to express in a courageous and clear way the real presence of the Lord, above all through the solemnity and the correctness of the celebrations.

I ask this in a special way of priests, about whom I am thinking in this moment with great affection. The priestly ministry was born in the Cenacle, together with the Eucharist, as my venerated predecessor John Paul II underlined so many times. "The priestly life must have in a special way a 'Eucharistic form'", he wrote in his last Letter for Holy Thursday. The devout daily celebration of Holy Mass, the centre of the life and mission of every priest, contributes to this end.

Nourished and sustained by the Eucharist, Catholics cannot but feel stimulated to tend towards that full unity for which Christ hoped in the Cenacle. Peter's Successor knows that he must take on this supreme desire of the Divine Master in a particularly special way. To him, indeed, has been entrusted the duty of strengthening his brethren.

Thus, in full awareness and at the beginning of his ministry in the Church of Rome that Peter bathed with his blood, the current Successor assumes as his primary commitment that of working tirelessly towards the reconstitution of the full and visible unity of all Christ's followers. This is his ambition, this is his compelling duty. He is aware that to do so, expressions of good feelings are not enough. Concrete gestures are required to penetrate souls and move consciences, encouraging everyone to that interior conversion which is the basis for all progress on the road of ecumenism.

Theological dialogue is necessary. A profound examination of the historical reasons behind past choices is also indispensable. But even more urgent is that "purification of memory" which was so often evoked by John Paul II, and which alone can dispose souls to welcome the full truth of Christ. It is before Him, supreme Judge of all living things, that each of us must stand, in the awareness that one day we must explain to Him what we did and what we did not do for the great good that is the full and visible unity of all His disciples.

The current Successor of Peter feels himself to be personally implicated in this question and is disposed to do all in his power to promote the fundamental cause of ecumenism. In the wake of his predecessors, he is fully determined to cultivate any initiative that may seem appropriate to promote contact and agreement with representatives from the various Churches and ecclesial communities. Indeed, on this occasion he sends them too his most cordial greetings in Christ, the one Lord of all.

In this moment, I go back in my memory to the unforgettable experience we all underwent with the death and the funeral of the lamented John Paul II. Around his mortal remains, lying on the bare earth, leaders of nations gathered, with people from all social classes and especially the young, in an unforgettable embrace of affection and admiration. The entire world looked to him with trust. To many it seemed as if that intense participation, amplified to the ends of the planet by the social communications media, was like a choral request for help addressed to the Pope by modern humanity which, wracked by fear and uncertainty, questions itself about the future.

The Church today must revive within herself an awareness of the task of presenting the world again with the voice of the One Who said: "I am the light of the world; he who follows me will not walk in darkness but will have the light of life." In undertaking his ministry, the new Pope knows that his task is to bring the light of Christ to shine before the men and women of today: not his own light but that of Christ.

With this awareness, I address myself to everyone, even to those who follow other religions or who are simply seeking an answer to the fundamental questions of life and have not yet found it. I address everyone with simplicity and affection, to assure them that the Church wants to continue to build an open and sincere dialogue with them, in a search for the true good of mankind and of society.

From God I invoke unity and peace for the human family and declare the willingness of all Catholics to cooperate for true social development, one that respects the dignity of all human beings.

I will make every effort and dedicate myself to pursuing the promising dialogue that my predecessors began with various civilizations, because it is mutual understanding that gives rise to conditions for a better future for everyone.

I am particularly thinking of young people. To them, the privileged interlocutors of John Paul II, I send an affectionate embrace in the hope, God willing, of meeting them at Cologne on the occasion of the next World Youth Day. With you, dear young people, I will continue to maintain a dialogue, listening to your expectations in an attempt to help you meet, ever more profoundly, the living, ever young, Christ.

"*Mane nobiscum, Domine!*" Stay with us Lord! This invocation, which forms the dominant theme of John Paul II's Apostolic Letter for the Year of the Eucharist, is the prayer that comes spontaneously from my heart as I turn to begin the ministry to which Christ has called me. Like Peter, I too renew to Him my unconditional promise of faithfulness. He alone I intend to serve as I dedicate myself totally to the service of His Church.

In support of this promise, I invoke the maternal intercession of Mary Most Holy, in whose hands I place the present and the future of my person and of the Church. May the Holy Apostles Peter and Paul, and all the saints, also intercede.

With these sentiments I impart to you, venerated brother cardinals, to those participating in this ritual, and to all those following it by television and radio, a special and affectionate blessing.

A panoramic view of St Peter's Square, the front of St Peter's Basilica, the Sistine Chapel and the Apostolic Palace (where the Pope lives), during the Inaugural Mass of Pope Benedict XVI, on Sunday 24 April 2005.

Photograph by Peter Jennings

Pope Benedict XVI receiving the Ring of the Fisherman from Cardinal Angelo Sodano during his Inaugural Mass in St Peter's Square, on Sunday 24 April 2005.

Fotografia Felici

Pope Benedict XVI delivering his homily during his Inaugural Mass.

Fotografia Felici

The Inaugural Mass of Benedict XVI

St Peter's Square, Sunday 24 April 2005

Pope Benedict XVI presided at the Eucharistic celebration for the official inauguration of his Petrine ministry, together with 150 cardinals, in St Peter's Square at 10 am on Sunday 24 April 2005, the Fifth Sunday of Easter. Among the bishops, priests and religious present was the Pope's brother, Mgr Georg Ratzinger.

Before the start of Mass the Pope, Benedict XVI, together with the patriarchs of the Oriental Churches, descended to the tomb of St Peter, below the papal altar (altar of the *Confessio*), and remained in prayer for a brief period.

He then incensed the tomb, during which time two deacons took a coffer containing the pastoral pallium and with the Ring of the Fisherman and the Book of Gospels processed outside the basilica to place them on the altar.

At the end of the Liturgy of the Word and the proclamation of the Gospel in both Latin and Greek, two deacons carried the pallium and the Ring of the Fisherman, from the altar to the chair of the Holy Father. They were joined by Cardinal Angelo Sodano, Cardinal Stephen Kim Sou-hwan and Cardinal Jorge Arturo Medina Estevez. Cardinal Medina Estevez, the Cardinal Proto-Deacon, then placed the petrine pallium on the shoulders of Benedict XVI.

The pallium is a very ancient episcopal symbol made of lamb's wool, which indicates the authority of a bishop and his link with the See of Peter. The petrine pallium is white and a mix of lamb's wool and sheep wool and is embroidered with five red crosses.

Cardinal Angelo Sodano, then placed the Ring of the Fisherman on the Holy Father's right hand. The ring given to Benedict XVI has the image seal of St Peter that authenticates the faith and marks the duty entrusted to Peter to confirm his brothers. The ring is also called the Ring of the Fisherman because the boat and net depicted upon it symbolize Peter the fisherman Apostle who, having believed the word of Jesus, cast his net out from the boat for a miraculous catch of fish.

After Pope Benedict XVI blessed the faithful, he returned to his seat where twelve people swore obedience – the three cardinals, a bishop, a priest, a deacon, a male and female religious, a married couple and two young people recently confirmed.

There were 141 delegations representing heads of State and governments in attendance at the celebration. There were also various religious delegations comprising a total of seventy people, including representatives from Orthodox Churches, Eastern Orthodox Churches (the ancient Churches of the East), Churches and Christian communities of the West, including the Archbishop of Canterbury, Dr Rowan Williams, head of the worldwide Anglican Communion.

Many of the people who filled the Via della Conciliazione, adjacent streets and other areas of Rome were able to follow the ceremony on giant screens.

Homily of Benedict XVI
at his Inaugural Mass

St Peter's Square, Sunday 24 April 2005

"Like Jesus, I will be a shepherd,

like Peter, a fisher of Men"

Your Eminences, my dear brother bishops and priests, distinguished authorities and members of the diplomatic corps, dear brothers and sisters.

During these days of great intensity, we have chanted the litany of the saints on three different occasions: at the funeral of our Holy Father John Paul II; as the cardinals entered the conclave; and again today, when we sang it with the response *"Tu illum adiuva"* – sustain the new Successor of St Peter. On each occasion, in a particular way, I found great consolation in listening to this prayerful chant. How alone we all felt after the passing of John Paul II – the Pope who for over twenty-six years had been our shepherd and guide in our journey through life! He crossed the threshold of the next life, entering into the mystery of God. But he did not take this step alone. Those who believe are never alone – neither in life nor in death. At that moment, we could call upon the saints from every age – his friends, his brothers and sisters in the faith – knowing that they would form a living procession to accompany him into the next world, into the glory of God. We knew that his arrival was awaited. Now we know that he is among his own and is truly at home.

We were also consoled as we made our solemn entrance into conclave, to elect the one whom the Lord had chosen. How would we be able to discern his name? How could 115 bishops, from every culture and every country, discover the one on whom the Lord wished to confer the mission of binding and loosing? Once again, we knew that we were not alone, we knew that we were surrounded, led and guided by the friends of God. And now, at this moment, weak servant of God that I am, I must assume this enormous task, which truly exceeds all human capacity. How can I do this? How will I be able to do it? All of you, my dear friends, have just invoked the entire host of saints, representing some of the great names in the history of God's dealings with mankind. In this way, I too can say with renewed conviction: I am not alone. I do not have to carry alone what in truth I could never carry alone. All the Saints of God are there to protect me, to sustain me and to carry me. And your prayers, my dear friends, your indulgence, your love, your faith and your hope accompany me. Indeed, the communion of saints consists not only of the great men and women who went before us and whose names we know. All of us belong to the communion of saints, we who have been baptized in the name of the Father and of the Son and of the Holy Spirit, we who draw life from the gift of Christ's Body and Blood, through which he transforms us and makes us like Himself.

Yes, the Church is alive - this is the wonderful experience of these days. During those sad days of the Pope's illness and death, it became wonderfully evident to us that the Church is alive. And the Church is young. She holds within herself the future of the world and therefore shows each of us the way towards the future. The Church is alive and we are seeing it: we are experiencing the joy that the Risen Lord promised his followers. The Church is alive – she is alive because Christ is alive, because he is truly risen. In the suffering that we saw on the Holy Father's face in those days of Easter, we contemplated the mystery of Christ's Passion and we touched his wounds. But throughout these days we have also been able, in a profound sense, to touch the Risen One. We have been able to experience the joy that he promised, after a brief period of darkness, as the fruit of His resurrection.

The Church is alive – with these words, I greet with great joy and gratitude all of you gathered here, my venerable brother cardinals and bishops, my dear priests, deacons, Church workers, catechists. I greet you, men and women religious, witnesses of the transfiguring presence of God. I greet you, members of the lay faithful, immersed in the great task of building up the Kingdom of God which spreads throughout the world, in every area of life. With great affection I also greet all those who have been reborn in the Sacrament of Baptism but are not yet in full communion with us; and you, my brothers and sisters of the Jewish people, to whom we are joined by a great shared spiritual heritage, one rooted in God's irrevocable promises. Finally, like a wave gathering force, my thoughts go out to all men and women of today, to believers and non-believers alike.

Dear friends! At this moment there is no need for me to present a program of governance. I was able to give an indication of what I see as my task in my Message of Wednesday 20 April, and there will be other opportunities to do so. My real programme of governance is not to do my own will, not to pursue my own ideas, but to listen, together with the whole Church, to the word and the will of the Lord, to be guided by him, so that he himself will lead the Church at this hour of our history. Instead of putting forward a programme, I should simply like to comment on the two liturgical symbols which represent the inauguration of the Petrine Ministry; both these symbols, moreover, reflect clearly what we heard proclaimed in today's readings.

The first symbol is the *pallium*, woven in pure wool, which will be placed on my shoulders. This ancient sign, which the bishops of Rome have worn since the fourth century, may be considered an image of the yoke of Christ, which the bishop of this city, the Servant of the Servants of God, takes upon his shoulders. God's yoke is God's will, which we accept. And this will does not weigh down on us, oppressing us and taking away our freedom. To know what God wants, to know where the path of life is found – this was Israel's joy, this was her great privilege. It is also our joy: God's will does not alienate us, it purifies us – even if this can be painful – and so it leads us to ourselves. In this way, we serve not only him, but the salvation of the whole world, of all history.

The symbolism of the pallium is even more concrete: the lamb's wool is meant to represent the lost, sick or weak sheep which the shepherd places on his shoulders and carries to the waters of life. For the Fathers of the Church, the parable of the lost sheep, which the shepherd seeks in the desert, was an image of the mystery of Christ and the Church. The human race – every one of us – is the sheep lost in the desert which no longer knows the way. The Son of God will not let this happen; He cannot abandon humanity in so wretched a condition. He leaps to his feet and abandons the glory of heaven, in order to go in search of the sheep and pursue it, all the way to the Cross. He takes it upon his shoulders and carries our humanity; he carries us all – he is the good shepherd who lays down his life for the sheep. What the pallium indicates first and foremost is that we are all carried by Christ. But at the same time it invites us to carry one another. Hence the pallium becomes a symbol of the shepherd's mission, of which the second reading and the Gospel speak. The pastor must be inspired by Christ's holy zeal: for him it is not a matter of indifference that so many people are living in the desert. And there are so many kinds of desert. There is the desert of poverty, the desert of hunger and thirst, the desert of abandonment, of loneliness, of destroyed love. There is the desert of darkness, the emptiness of souls no longer aware of their dignity or the goal of human life. The external deserts in the world are growing, because the internal deserts have become so vast. Therefore the earth's treasures no longer serve to build God's garden for all to live in, but they have been made to serve the powers of exploitation and destruction. The Church as a whole, and all her pastors, like Christ must set out to lead people out of the desert, towards the place of life, towards friendship with the Son of God, towards the One who gives us life, and life in abundance.

The symbol of the lamb also has a deeper meaning. In the ancient Near East, it was customary for kings to style themselves shepherds of their people. This was an image of their power, a cynical image: to them their subjects were like sheep, which the shepherd could dispose of as he wished. When the shepherd of all humanity, the living God, himself became a lamb, he stood on the side of the lambs, with those who are downtrodden and killed. This is how he reveals himself to be the true shepherd: "I am the Good Shepherd ... I lay down my life for the sheep," Jesus says of himself (Jn 10:14ff). It is not power but love that redeems us! This is God's sign: he himself is love. How often we wish that God would show himself stronger, that he would strike decisively, defeating evil and creating a better world. All ideologies of power justify themselves in exactly this way, they justify the destruction of whatever would stand in the way of progress and the liberation of humanity. We suffer on account of God's patience. And yet, we need his patience. God, who became a lamb, tells us that the world is saved by the Crucified One, not by those who crucified Him. The world is redeemed by the patience of God. It is destroyed by the impatience of man.

One of the basic characteristics of a shepherd must be to love the people entrusted to him, even as he loves Christ whom he serves. "Feed my sheep" says Christ to Peter, and now, at this moment, he says it to me as well. Feeding means loving, and loving also means being ready to suffer. Loving means giving the sheep what is truly good, the nourishment of God's truth, of God's word, the nourishment of his presence, which he gives us in the blessed Sacrament. My dear friends – at this moment I can only say: pray for me, that I may learn to love the Lord more and more. Pray for me, that I may learn to love his flock more and more – in other words, you, the holy Church, each one of you and all of you together. Pray for me, that I may not flee for fear of the wolves. Let us pray for one another, that the Lord will carry us and that we will learn to carry one another.

The second symbol used in today's liturgy to express the inauguration of the Petrine ministry is the presentation of the *fisherman's ring*. Peter's call to be a shepherd, which we heard in the Gospel, comes after the account of a miraculous catch of fish: after a night in which the disciples had let down their nets without success, they see the Risen Lord on the shore. He tells them to let down their nets once more, and the nets become so full that they can hardly pull them in; 153 large fish, "and although there were so many, the net was not torn" (Jn 21:11). This account, coming at the end of Jesus' earthly journey with his disciples, corresponds to an account found at the beginning: there too, the disciples had caught nothing the entire night; there too, Jesus had invited Simon once more to put out into the deep. And Simon, who was not yet called Peter, gave the wonderful reply: "Master, at your word I will let down the nets." And then came the conferral of his mission: "Do not be afraid. Henceforth you will be catching men" (Lk 5:1-11). Today too the Church and the successors of the Apostles are told to put out into the deep sea of history and to let down the nets, so as to win men and women over to the Gospel – to God, to Christ, to true life. The Fathers made a very significant commentary on this singular task. This is what they say: for a fish, created for water, it is fatal to be taken out of the sea, to be removed from its vital element to serve as human food. But in the mission of a fisher of men, the reverse is true. We are living in alienation, in the salt waters of suffering and death; in a sea of darkness without light. The net of the Gospel pulls us out of the waters of death and brings us into the splendor of God's light, into true life. It is really true: as we follow Christ in this mission to be fishers of men, we must bring men and women out of the sea that is salted with so many forms of alienation and onto the land of life, into the light of God.

It is really so: the purpose of our lives is to reveal God to men. And only where God is seen does life truly begin. Only when we meet the living God in Christ do we know what life is. We are not some casual and meaningless product of evolution. Each of us is the result of a thought of God. Each of us is willed, each of us is loved, each of us is necessary. There is nothing more beautiful than to be surprised by the Gospel, by the encounter with Christ. There is nothing more beautiful than to know Him and to speak to others of our friendship with him. The task of the shepherd, the task of the fisher of men, can often seem wearisome. But it is beautiful and wonderful, because it is truly a service to joy, to God's joy which longs to break into the world.

Here I want to add something: both the image of the shepherd and that of the fisherman issue an explicit call to unity. "I have other sheep that are not of this fold; I must lead them too, and they will heed my voice. So there shall be one flock, one shepherd" (Jn 10:16); these are the words of Jesus at the end of His discourse on the Good Shepherd. And the account of the 153 large fish ends with the joyful statement: "although there were so many, the net was not torn" (Jn 21:11). Alas, beloved Lord, with sorrow we must now acknowledge that it has been torn! But no – we must not be sad! Let us rejoice because of your promise, which does not disappoint, and let us do all we can to pursue the path towards the unity you have promised. Let us remember it in our prayer to the Lord, as we plead with him: yes, Lord, remember your promise. Grant that we may be one flock and one shepherd! Do not allow Your net to be torn, help us to be servants of unity!

At this point, my mind goes back to 22 October 1978, when Pope John Paul II began his ministry here in Saint Peter's Square. His words on that occasion constantly echo in my ears: "Do not be afraid! Open wide the doors for Christ!" The Pope was addressing the mighty, the powerful of this world, who feared that Christ might take away something of their power if they were to let him in, if they were to allow the faith to be free. Yes, he would certainly have taken something away from them: the dominion of corruption, the manipulation of law and the freedom to do as they pleased. But he would not have taken away anything that pertains to human freedom or dignity, or to the building of a just society. The Pope was also speaking to everyone, especially the young. Are we not perhaps all afraid in some way? If we let Christ enter fully into our lives, if we open ourselves totally to him, are we not afraid that he might take something away from us? Are we not perhaps afraid to give up something significant, something unique, something that makes life so beautiful? Do we not then risk ending up diminished and deprived of our freedom? And once again the Pope said: No! If we let Christ into our lives, we lose nothing, nothing, absolutely nothing of what makes life free, beautiful and great. No! Only in this friendship are the doors of life opened wide. Only in this friendship is the great potential of human existence truly revealed. Only in this friendship do we experience beauty and liberation. And so, today, with great strength and great conviction, on the basis of long personal experience of life, I say to you, dear young people: Do not be afraid of Christ! He takes nothing away, and he gives you everything. When we give ourselves to him, we receive a hundred-fold in return. Yes, open, open wide the doors to Christ – and you will find true life. Amen.

Cardinal Newman, the last photograph, taken early in 1890. Newman is looking
out into the garden from the corridor between the Refectory and the Recreation
Room at the Oratory House, Birmingham.

Courtesy of the Fathers of the Birmingham Oratory

A Meditation by Cardinal Newman

God has created me to do him some definite service; he has committed some work to me which he has not committed to another. I have my mission - I may never know it in this life, but I shall be told it in the next.

I am a link in a chain, a bond of connection between persons. He has not created me for naught. I shall do good, I shall do his work; I shall be an angel of peace, a preacher of truth in my own place, while not intending it, if I do but keep his commandments and serve him in my calling.

Therefore I will trust him. Whatever, wherever I am, I can never be thrown away. If I am in sickness, my sickness may serve him; in perplexity, my perplexity may serve him; if I am in sorrow, my sorrow may serve him. My sickness, or perplexity, or sorrow may be necessary causes of some great end, which is quite beyond us. He does nothing in vain; he may prolong my life, he may shorten it; he knows what he is about. He may take away my friends, he may throw me among strangers, he may make me feel desolate, make my spirits sink, hide my future from me – still he knows what he is about.

Meditations and Devotions, written by Cardinal Newman during the 1850s for the boys of the Oratory School, published in 1893. This prayer is taken from 'Meditations on Christian Doctrine'.

About the Contributors

CARDINAL JOSEPH RATZINGER, now POPE BENEDICT XVI. Prefect of the Congregation for the Doctrine of the Faith, 1981 to 2 April 2005. Appointed Dean of the College of Cardinals by Pope John Paul II in 2002, he was elected Bishop of Rome and Successor of St Peter on 19 April 2005. He took the name Pope Benedict XVI.

CARDINAL CORMAC MURPHY-O'CONNOR, Archbishop of Westminster, and President of the Bishops' Conference of England and Wales. Born Reading, Berkshire, 24 August 1932. Appointed Bishop of Arundel and Brighton in 1977. Pope John Paul II appointed him Archbishop of Westminster in February 2000. He took part in the Conclave that elected Pope Benedict XVI.

CARDINAL EDWARD CASSIDY was President of the Pontifical Council for Promoting Christian Unity, 1989 to 2001. Born Sydney, Australia, 5 July 1924.

CARDINAL JEAN-MARIE LUSTIGER was Archbishop of Paris, 1981 to February 2005. Born Paris, 17 September 1926. His parents were Jewish shopkeepers and had come from Poland. He took part in the Conclave that elected Pope Benedict XVI.

CARDINAL ALFONS MARIA STICKLER SDB was Archivist of the Vatican Secret Archives and Librarian of the Vatican Library, from 1985 to 1988. Born Austria, 23 August 1910. Pope John Paul II created him a Cardinal Deacon in May 1985, giving him the deaconry of S. Giorgio in Velabro, Cardinal Newman's Titular Church in Rome.

ARCHBISHOP VINCENT NICHOLS was born in Crosby, Liverpool, 8 November 1945. Was appointed as the first General Secretary of the Bishops' Conference of England and Wales in 1984, and an Auxiliary Bishop in the Archdiocese of Westminster in 1992. Pope John Paul II appointed him as the eighth Archbishop of Birmingham in February 2000.

BISHOP PHILIP BOYCE OCD, of Raphoe. Born County Donegal, Ireland, 25 January 1940. A Discalced Carmelite, he wrote his doctoral thesis on the Spirituality of Cardinal John Henry Newman. Pope John Paul II appointed this Newman scholar Bishop of Raphoe, in June 1995.

FR PAUL CHAVASSE was born in Wolverhampton, Staffordshire, 31 January 1954. He joined the Birmingham Oratory in 1980, and was appointed Provost on 2 February 1992. He was elected Postulator of the Cause of the Venerable John Henry Cardinal Newman in 2002.

FR STEPHEN DESSAIN, 1907-1976, a great Newman scholar, was Archivist of the Birmingham Oratory, and Editor of *The Letters and Diaries of John Henry Newman* 1958-1976. Born Dorking, Surrey, 2 September 1907. He joined the Oratory in 1929 and was Provost from 1956 to 1962. He died suddenly, 31 May 1976, aged 68.

FR GREGORY WINTERTON served as Provost of the Birmingham Oratory from 1971 to 1992, holding office longer than anyone other than Newman himself. Born Brighton, 9 July 1922. Like Newman he was a clergyman in the Church of England before being received into the Catholic Church in 1955. He joined the Oratory in 1961 and was ordained a priest on 9 March 1963. He was elected Provost for the first time on 2 February 1971 and in the mid-1970's he helped to revive popular interest in Cardinal Newman, and inspired the foundation of the *Friends of Cardinal Newman.*

FR VINCENT BLEHL S J, 1921-2001. In 1980 the Fathers of the Birmingham Oratory appointed him Chairman of the Historical Commission set up to examine Newman's life, virtues and reputation for holiness. In 1986 he was appointed Postulator of the Newman Cause and was responsible for drawing up the *Positio.* He died on 14 November 2001, aged 80.

ABBOT CUTHBERT JOHNSON OSB, of Quarr Abbey, Isle of Wight. Born Hebburn County Durham, 11 July 1946, Feast of St Benedict, Patron of Europe. He worked as an official in the Congregation for Divine Worship and the Discipline of the Sacraments in Rome from 1983 until he was elected Abbot on 22 August 1996.

DR GEOFFREY ROWELL, DD, was appointed Anglican Bishop of Gibraltar in Europe in 2004. Born 13 February 1943. He was chaplain at Keble College Oxford 1972 to 1994.

Recommended Internet Resources

www.newmanreader.org	The Newman Reader
www.indcatholicnews.com	Independent Catholic News
www.vatican.va	The official Vatican website
www.zenit.org	Zenit International News Agency
www.newmanfriendsinternational.org	International Centre of Newman Friends

Peter Jennings, Editor

Peter Jennings was born in London on 4 December 1947 and baptised in 1948 at the Birmingham Oratory by the great Newman scholar, Fr Stephen Dessain. He has written and broadcast extensively about the Catholic Church and the Vatican since the late 1970s. During April 2005 he gave a number of television and radio interviews from Rome during the Conclave and the Inaugural Mass of Pope Benedict XVI.

He is author of *The Pope In Britain*, the Official Record of the pastoral visit of Pope John Paul II to Great Britain in 1982. A correspondent for *Our Sunday Visitor*, 1986-91, he is Press Secretary to the Most Reverend Vincent Nichols, Archbishop of Birmingham, and the Archdiocese of Birmingham. He is also Press Secretary for Quarr Abbey, Isle of Wight, and the Benedictine Congregation of Solesmes in England. He is a member of the Executive Committee of the *Friends of Cardinal Newman*.

His publications include: *Aerogrammes*, 1973; *Face to Face with the Turin Shroud* (ed.), 1978; *The Come Sunday Book*, 1979; *The Church 2001* (ed.), 1982; *An End to Terrorism*, 1984; *Children of the Troubles* (ed.), 1986; *The Queen Mother's Century Celebrated in Stamps*, 2000.

On 17 August 1995 he suffered a massive sub-arachnoid brain hemorrhage while on a family holiday in Anglesey, North Wales. He was given the Sacrament of the Sick and doctors told his wife, Stella, that he only had a five per cent chance of survival. In early September, shortly after he regained consciousness, Fr Gregory Winterton, former Provost of the Birmingham Oratory, 1971-92, who revived the Cause of John Henry Newman, blessed Peter with the relic of St Philip Neri, founder of the Congregation of the Oratory. He felt the fuzziness inside his head clear. Father Winterton blessed him with the relic a second time 48 hours later and his head cleared completely. He has made a remarkable recovery.

A Fellow of the Royal Philatelic Society London, and the Royal Geographical Society, and a member of the Club de Monte-Carlo de l'Elite de la Philatélie; Peter Jennings is also well known for his writing about postage stamps and the engaging hobby of philately.

He and his wife Stella live in Birmingham. They have two grown up children, Sarah and Joseph.

Acknowledgements

I owe a great debt of gratitude to the Fathers of Cardinal Newman's Birmingham Oratory, past and present. In particular to Fr Stephen Dessain, the great Newman scholar; to Fr Basil Lynch, 1906-1991; to Fr Humphrey Crookenden, 1908-1978; and to Fr Michael Day, 1920-2003. I have been privileged to work on many projects with Fr Gregory Winterton, from the time he was first elected Provost in 1971, to help raise popular awareness of Cardinal Newman through the media. His encouragement, support and advice over the years have been invaluable. I am also most grateful to his successor as Provost, Fr Paul Chavasse, a good friend, for his help and encouragement during the editing of this book; and to Br Lewis Berry, a novice at the Birmingham Oratory, for his meticulous work in helping to correct the final typescript. The Fathers have kindly allowed me to go through their photographic archives and select the sketches, portraits and a number of little known photographs of their founder, for inclusion in this volume.

Several people in Rome have given me generous help over a period of many years. These include: Archbishop John P Foley, President of the Pontifical Council for Social Communications; and in the Holy See Press Office, Dr Joaquin Navarro-Valls, Director, Fr Ciro Benedettini CP, Vice-Director, and Sister Giovanna Gentili, Accreditation. Special thanks are due to Arturo Mari, the distinguished photographer from *L'Osservatore Romano*, whom I have known for more than a quarter of a century, and also to Federico Felici and Rodolfo Felici of Fotografia Felici. I am also grateful to Sister Maria Pinto, of the International Focolare Movement in Rome. I am especially grateful to Sister Irene Felder FSO and Sister Mary Dechant FSO at the International Centre of Newman Friends in Rome and at The College in Littlemore Oxford, both members of the Spiritual Family The Work.

I am extremely grateful to Cardinal Cormac Murphy-O'Connor, Archbishop of Westminster, for his contribution to this volume, 'The Importance of Cardinal Newman Today'; to Archbishop Vincent Nichols of Birmingham, who has taken a keen interest as I have researched and edited this work. His contribution 'Newman's Pastoral Work in Birmingham' is much appreciated. To Abbot Cuthbert Johnson OSB, of Quarr Abbey for his 'monastic' contribution; to author and journalist Greg Watts, who listened attentively to my initial ideas for this book in Rome during April 2005. I should like to thank Denis Riches, Director of Family Publications in Oxford, and his colleagues. Denis's advice, and suggestions, from the time he received my manuscript until the completion of this book, have been invaluable.

Finally, a most sincere thank you to my long-suffering wife Stella and children, now grown up, Sarah and Joseph, for their tolerance, forbearance and love during this and many other projects.